NAVIGATING RIGHT
AND WRONG

NAVIGATING RIGHT AND WRONG

ETHICAL DECISION MAKING IN A PLURALISTIC AGE

DANIEL E. LEE

ROWMAN & LITTLEFIELD PUBLISHERS, INC.
Lanham • Boulder • New York • Oxford

ROWMAN & LITTLEFIELD PUBLISHERS, INC.

Published in the United States of America
by Rowman & Littlefield Publishers, Inc.
A Member of the Rowman & Littlefield Publishing Group
4720 Boston Way, Lanham, Maryland 20706
www.rowmanlittlefield.com

PO Box 317
Oxford
OX2 9RU, UK

British Library Cataloguing in Publication Information Available

Library of Congress Cataloging-in-Publication Data

Lee, Daniel E.
    Navigating right and wrong : ethical decision making in a pluralistic
age / Daniel E. Lee.
        p.   cm.
Includes bibliographical references and index.
    ISBN 0-7425-1394-7 (alk. paper) — ISBN 0-7425-1395-5 (pbk. : alk.
paper)
    1. Ethics.   I. Title.
    BJ1012 .L42   2002
    170—dc21

                                                                        2002006967

Printed in the United States of America

♾ ™The paper used in this publication meets the minimum requirements of
American National Standard for Information Sciences—Permanence of Paper
for Printed Library Materials, ANSI/NISO Z39.48–1992.

CONTENTS

—

PREFACE

—

It was once so easy. The question "What ought I do?" was very simply answered by referring to the teachings of the church, synagogue, temple, or mosque that one attended or by seeking guidance from parents, priests, rabbis, or teachers. Without hesitation, folks would talk about their obligations to their families, to their employers, to their communities, and to their country. Young men talked about various ways of fulfilling their "military obligation" without in any way questioning whether there indeed was such an obligation. Duty, obligation, and service to one's family, community, and country were, in substantial measure, the coin of the realm.

And then it all changed as the 1960s witnessed widespread rejection of traditional values and notions of authority. We have been trying to sort out the pieces ever since.[1]

I began wrestling with these matters while an undergraduate, wondering whether there really is anything that definitively can be said to be right or wrong and whether there is any meaningful way in which we can talk about duty and obligation. Concern about these matters was, in no small measure, the reason I chose to pursue graduate studies in ethics. My doctoral dissertation, which was the beginning of the intellectual odyssey that a quarter of a century later has given rise to this volume, focused attention on questions of obligation as they pertained to the law. There was a reason for that. If there is any case to be made for duty or obligation, it seemed to me that the case ought to be easiest to make with respect to complying with the laws enacted by our governing bodies on the federal, state, and local levels. There is a certain minimalist ethic—held by some in the business world, for example—that suggests that we are free to do whatever we wish to do, as long as it isn't illegal. Moreover, a rich and varied body of literature, both philosophical and theological, addresses questions of obligation related to the law. Hence, I surmised, if a case was to be made for duty or obligation in an age that had experienced the demise of authority, perhaps it could be found in the philosophical and theological literature dealing with questions of law and obligation.

I had hoped to find some sort of basis for obligation, somewhere on which to stand and move the whole world. But in that endeavor I failed. The best that could be said for the conclusions I reached was that they were sufficiently plausible to satisfy the review committee at Yale University that had to approve my dissertation if I was to receive my degree. The review process, I might add, did have the salutary effect of reminding me that authority had not entirely disappeared from my life, even as it further stimulated my thinking about the matters with which I was wrestling.

Still not satisfied with the conclusions I had reached—not because I thought they were mistaken, but rather because they seemed incomplete—I returned to these matters in the late 1970s while a fellow at the National Humanities Institute at the University of Chicago. Then I put the project aside while teaching and writing other books, returning to some of the issues briefly while writing *Hope Is Where We Least Expect to Find It*, published in 1993.[2]

As did my dissertation, the present volume uses the question of whether there is an obligation to comply with the law as a means of getting at the question of what might be the nature of ethics, in general, and obligation, in particular. While my conclusions have not changed significantly from those I reached a quarter of a century ago, I now have an increased awareness of both the breadth and the complexity of these issues and a growing awareness of how much there is that we don't know. As a result, the pages that follow go far beyond anything I could have written while a graduate student in the late 1960s and early 1970s. And it is addressed to a broader audience—not just those in the academic world but also the thoughtful members of the general public who have struggled, as I have, with questions of right and wrong, duty and obligation, in a world that doesn't always seem to make sense.

This volume is intended to be used in the classroom, not as the sole text for a course, but rather as a concise work that might be used along with other assigned reading. It is also my hope that the volume will be of interest to book clubs, those attending retreats of various sorts, adult education classes at churches and synagogues, and members of the general public who enjoy reading serious books written in a readable manner. The volume does not assume any prior knowledge about ethical theory or about particular theologians or philosophers.

While reference is made to a number of theologians and philosophers, this is not a book about any of them. Rather, the focus is on certain basic questions of significance for the way we might make moral judgments and understand questions of obligation in this age of pluralism. Those wishing to know more about the theologians and philosophers to whom reference is made should read their writings. The notes at the end of each chapter can be helpful in pointing the reader in the direction of relevant passages.

Finally, I wish to note that this volume is not for everyone. Those unwilling to "think outside the box" are not likely to be pleased with the arguments made in the pages that follow because they challenge numerous widely held assumptions. Those who fancy that they have a "God's-eye" view of the truth or otherwise believe that they have all-encompassing answers to ethical questions will probably take sharp exception to what I say about these matters. So be it. Sometimes being uncomfortable is the first step toward creative thinking.

During orientation week at the beginning of my first year of college, the chaplain noted that many of us had probably arrived there expecting to find answers to our questions. "I've got to tell you, though," he continued, "that when you graduate from here four years from now, you'll have far more questions than answers." He was right about that. This book is for those who are willing to question conventional wisdom, look beyond what is widely assumed to be the case, and wrestle with questions of the most untidy sort.

I did part of the work on the manuscript while on sabbatical during spring term of the 2001–2 academic year; I am appreciative of Augustana College for providing sabbatical support. I am greatly indebted to the following individuals who read drafts of this volume, either in part or in whole, and made numerous helpful suggestions: Christopher Annis, Robert Benne, Lendol Calder, Thomas Sieger Derr, Ellen Hay, Jan Keessen, Peter Kivisto, Joseph McCaffrey, Jayne Rose, Caroline Skaggs, Holly Yoshinari, and Karin Youngberg. I am also deeply appreciative of the suggestions made by the two anonymous reviewers and by Eve M. DeVaro, associate editor for acquisitions in philosophy at Rowman & Littlefield Publishers, and of the copyediting and proofreading done by Lawrence Paulson and Cheryl Hoffman. Any remaining errors are, of course, solely my responsibility and should in no way be blamed on those who were kind enough to read the manuscript and share with me their thoughts and suggestions.

NOTES

1. I in no way wish to suggest that chaos and confusion were all that came out of the 1960s. There was a lot good that happened as well—the civil rights movement, the equal rights movement, the environmental movement, and much more.

2. Daniel E. Lee, *Hope Is Where We Least Expect to Find It* (Lanham, Md.: University Press of America, 1993).

INTRODUCTION

—

Nearly eight centuries ago, the distinguished Dominican philosopher and theologian Thomas Aquinas (1224/25–74) suggested that unjust laws "do not bind in conscience."[1] Half a millennium later, Martin Luther King Jr. (1929–68), writing from the confines of the city jail in Birmingham, Alabama, where he had been imprisoned for parading without a permit, made reference to Aquinas in distinguishing two basic types of laws: just laws and unjust laws. King wrote, "A just law is a man-made code that squares with the moral law or the law of God. An unjust law is a code that is out of harmony with moral law." Like Aquinas, King argued that unjust laws are not binding on conscience.[2]

Though appealing in its simplicity, the claim that any obligation (or lack thereof) to obey a particular law derives from its moral content (or lack thereof) is problematic in an age of ethical pluralism. As will be noted in chapter 2, there are many different styles of ethical decision making incorporating many different sets of values. We live in times in which there are all sorts of divergent views as to what is right and wrong, about what we ought to do and what we ought to refrain from doing.

The approach espoused by Aquinas and King works best if one can speak with confidence of an existing moral order in the universe and, with appeals to this existing moral order, argue that some moral claims are right while others are false or mistaken. But therein lies a dilemma, for it is far easier to assert that there is an existing moral order in the universe than it is to give a plausible explanation of how we might go about determining the structure and content of this moral order. To put this in slightly different words, it is one thing to believe that there is an existing moral order in the universe. It is quite another matter to attempt to come up with any sort of persuasive proof that such is the case.

Aquinas and the others who have asserted that there is an existing moral order in the universe, of course, have not been oblivious to this matter. Some have suggested that we can discover things of ethical significance in nature if we look carefully at the world that surrounds us. Others insist that we are born with built-in moral instincts, perhaps in the form of a conscience with which we are endowed from birth. Some suggest that there are certain moral truths that are self-evident if we simply think about them enough. Still others say, "All of the above."

All of that would be fine were it not, as will be noted in chapter 3, that there are significant problems with all of these approaches. Once we come to grips with these difficulties and limitations, we are essentially left with two choices. One option is subjectivism, the view that ethical values do not exist apart from human decisions and that there is nothing apart from personal preference to suggest that one set of ethical values is in any way superior to any other. In short, subjectivism in ethics is the ethical equivalent of the view that "beauty is in the eye of the beholder." The other option is a faith-based approach that characterizes the values we espouse as part of the faith we affirm, be it a faith that is religiously based or a faith that is entirely secular in nature. I am inclined toward the faith-based approach to ethics. In saying this, I fully recognize that when all things are considered, I can do no more than simply say that I firmly believe that there really are some things that are right and some things that are wrong, as given expression in the faith I affirm.

But if ethical questions are to be addressed within a framework of faith, such an approach comes equipped with its own set of problems. A recurring tragedy of history is that those who presume to speak from the perspective of faith have often falsely assumed that they have had a God's-eye view of the truth as they have gone around passing judgment on everyone in sight. What is presumed to be faith can very easily become arrogance. During the Spanish Inquisition and on other occasions in the course of history, thousands of lives have been snuffed out in the name of faith, suffering perpetrated by persecutors who failed to understand the true nature of faith

To assume falsely that one has a God's-eye view of the truth is to misunderstand grotesquely the nature of faith. As will be argued in chapter 4, faith, properly understood, must begin with humility—with the realization and acknowledgment that we don't have all the answers. There is much that we don't understand, much that is beyond the capacity of reason as we know and experience it. In short, faith is not a quick trip to the top of a mountain.

The practical impact of this understanding of faith is that it places ethics on a horizontal rather than a vertical axis. We are not privileged to view the world and all that exists from the top of some high mountain. Rather, we live in the valley below. Try though we might, our finiteness is such that we cannot by dint of faith or reason find a place on which to stand and move the whole world. To imagine otherwise is to succumb to vanity that gives rise to arrogance.

And so we must disabuse ourselves of the pretensions that all too often distort our vision. We must not only recognize that we live in the valley below but also, and even more important, learn how to live in this valley. As will be noted in chapter 5, a faith-based ethic set on a horizontal axis involves opening our eyes to the humanity of others, listening carefully to their cares and concerns in an open-minded manner, understanding their fears and anxieties, and being responsive to their needs. It involves seeing the persons behind what we perceive as faults, thereby enabling us to relate to them as fellow human beings rather than as objects of scorn and condescension.

Back to where we began. Where does this leave us with respect to a theory of obligation pertaining to the law? Once we come to grips with the fact that neither faith nor reason gets us to the top of the mountain, the only claims of obligation we can make derive from values rooted in the particular faith that we affirm, be it religiously based or entirely secular in nature. As will be noted in chapter 6, the American naturalist and philosopher Henry David Thoreau (1817–62) was pretty close to being right when he stated that "the only obligation which I have a right to assume, is to do at any time what I think is right."[3]

But if such an individualistic approach to ethics is taken, is there any meaningful way in which we can speak of others having obligations? One person's faith is hardly a sufficient basis for another person's condemnation. After all, that is precisely what went wrong during the Spanish Inquisition and on numerous other occasions destructive of the humanity of others. If we are to make claims of obligation pertaining to others, all that we can do is reach out on a horizontal plane by attempting to identify common values to which reference can be made. If it is the values to which we are committed that bind us in conscience, the same is true of others as well; the values to which they are committed are what bind them in conscience. It is unlikely, of course, that we would be inclined to argue that others should do things at odds with the values we affirm. Thus we must attempt to identify common values if we are to make claims of obligation pertaining to others that go beyond merely expressing an opinion as to what they ought to do.

Granted, the very nature of ethical pluralism is such that we should not presume that it is possible to identify all-encompassing values affirmed by all those whose lives intersect with ours. This, however, should not deter us from attempting to find agreement when such exists. Nor does it preclude proclaiming as worthy of consideration values that we hold dear.

Tidy this is not. Nor does it get us to the top of a mountain where, driven by the vanities that afflict us, we fancy that we belong. But is there not something to be said for realism rather than flights of fancy? For recognizing who we are and what we are capable of doing rather than being pretentious? For reaching out and responding to the humanity of others rather than presumptuously taking it upon ourselves to stand in judgment of them?

NOTES

1. Thomas Aquinas, *Summa Theologica,* trans. Fathers of the English Dominican Province (New York: Benziger, 1947), I-II, Q.96, A.3.

2. Martin Luther King Jr., "Letter from Birmingham Jail," in *Why We Can't Wait* (New York: Signet Books, 1964), 82.

3. Henry David Thoreau, "Civil Disobedience," in *Civil Disobedience: Theory and Practice,* ed. Hugo Adam Bedau (Indianapolis: Bobbs-Merrill, 1969), 28.

1

"WITHOUT JUSTICE, WHAT ARE KINGDOMS

BUT GREAT ROBBERIES?"

In the early 1960s, Birmingham, Alabama, was not the sort of place anyone who believed in human decency was comfortable visiting. A century had passed since the Emancipation Proclamation had declared that all slaves in Alabama and the other states of the Confederacy that were in rebellion were "thenceforward and forever free." Nearly a century had passed since the Thirteenth Amendment to the U.S. Constitution banned slavery in all states of the Union. But in blatant disregard of both the content and the spirit of the Emancipation Proclamation and the Thirteenth Amendment, the "Jim Crow" laws of the South held in bondage the African American children and grandchildren of slaves and former slaves by subjecting them to the most humiliating forms of treatment imaginable. In Birmingham, the largest industrial city in a state in which Governor George Wallace had vowed there would be "segregation now, segregation tomorrow, segregation forever," African Americans were barred from parks, restaurants, and movie theaters reserved for whites. They were denied jobs that might provide a decent standard of living for their families and educational opportunities that might enable better lives for them and for their children. These troubled years had witnessed the bombing of numerous

African American churches and the homes of civil rights leaders—bombings that officially remained "unsolved." Mutilated bodies of African Americans were found abandoned along lonely roads. Brutality ran rampant.[1]

Eugene "Bull" Connor, Birmingham's commissioner of public safety, wasn't particularly concerned about the bombings or other acts of violence directed against African Americans. Public safety, as he practiced it, didn't encompass the entire population. An outspoken segregationist from whose mouth demeaning racial epithets spewed forth in profusion, Connor saw his job as keeping African Americans "in their place" and didn't hesitate to use high-pressure water hoses and police dogs to go after anyone who seemed to him to be getting out of line.

Fred Shuttlesworth, an Alabama native who served as pastor of Bethel Baptist Church in Birmingham and as head of the Birmingham affiliate of the Southern Christian Leadership Conference, was nearly killed when a bomb blew up his home on Christmas night, a night that is supposed to symbolize peace and goodwill. Declaring that "I wasn't saved to run," Shuttlesworth continued his efforts to desegregate Birmingham's buses, schools, and parks. A bomb blew up his church. Undeterred, Shuttlesworth and his wife attempted to enroll their children in a white school, an action that, in the wake of the U.S. Supreme Court's 1954 decision declaring segregated schools unconstitutional, should have been possible. A mob beat him with chains and brass knuckles and stabbed his wife in the hip. Still he persisted in his fight to end segregation because, as he put it, segregation "wasn't just gon' die away."[2]

In 1963, Shuttlesworth invited Martin Luther King Jr., the president of the Southern Christian Leadership Conference, to assist in the struggle. King organized a boycott that was initiated shortly before Easter. The boycott targeted white merchants unwilling to hire or serve African Americans. Carefully chosen and trained demonstrators took seats at lunch counters reserved for whites. Birmingham police arrested them for "trespass after warning." Other demonstrators marched toward city hall, until Connor's uniformed officers stopped them. Refusing Connor's orders to disperse, they were arrested for "parading without a permit." City officials obtained a court injunction directing the protestors to cease their activities.

"Two days later," King recalled, "we did an audacious thing, something we had never done in any other crusade. We disobeyed a court order."[3] On Good Friday, after much discussion and prayer, King, joined by Ralph Abernathy and other leaders of the Southern Christian Leadership Conference, marched in defiance of the court injunction. Connor ordered their arrest. Two burly police officers dragged off King and Abernathy, clutching them by the backs of their shirts. King was placed in solitary confinement until, after intervention by Attorney General Robert Kennedy, he was finally allowed to meet with his lawyers and call his wife, who had recently given birth to their fourth child.

While King was in jail, a letter to the editor appeared in the *Birmingham News*, signed by eight prominent members of the clergy. Characterizing King's efforts in Birmingham as "unwise and untimely," the letter praised Birmingham police for their restraint and urged local African Americans to disengage from the protests, which, the letter claimed, were run by "outsiders." The letter encouraged African Americans instead to pursue their concerns in court.

When King was shown a copy of the letter four days after it ran, he decided that he needed to reply to it. Using a pen smuggled in by one of his lawyers to write on the margins of the newspaper containing the letter and on toilet tissue and scraps of paper supplied by a sympathetic fellow prisoner, King drafted what became one of his best-known writings, his "Letter from Birmingham Jail."

King noted that he was in Birmingham because he was invited to be there, adding that "injustice anywhere is a threat to justice everywhere." He further noted that negotiations with city officials had been attempted but had failed because of the unwillingness of city officials to negotiate in good faith. Then, getting to the crux of the matter. King allowed that "anxiety over our willingness to break laws" was a legitimate concern, adding that he and his associates "diligently urge people to obey the Supreme Court's decision of 1954 outlawing segregation in the public schools." But, then, why break some laws while urging compliance with other laws? King continued, "The answer lies in the fact that there are two types of laws: just and unjust. I would be the first to advocate obeying just laws. One has not only a legal but also a moral responsibility to obey just laws. Conversely, one has a moral responsibility to disobey unjust laws. I would agree with St. Augustine that 'an unjust law is no law at all.'"[4]

A CENTURIES-OLD SCHOOL OF THOUGHT

In arguing that we are not obligated to obey unjust laws, King was drawing upon a centuries-old school of thought that holds that a higher moral law stands in judgment of human laws and that any obligation to obey human laws is contingent on the moral content of those laws. Augustine (354–430), an early Christian bishop and theologian who prior to his conversion to Christianity lived a rather freewheeling lifestyle with few discernible moral standards, was by no means the only one to make this argument.[5] It was made with even greater forcefulness several centuries later by Thomas Aquinas, an Italian-born Dominican scholar whose influence on Roman Catholic thought is unequaled by any other theologian or philosopher, with the possible exception of Augustine, and whose influence extends to the thought of others, including King. Quoting Augustine, Aquinas spoke of unjust laws that are "acts of violence rather than laws." He added, "Wherefore such laws do not bind in conscience, except perhaps in order to avoid scandal or disturbance."[6]

The distinguished eighteenth-century English jurist and legal histo-

4

rian Sir William Blackstone (1723–80), whose *Commentaries on the Laws of England* played a key role in the education of several generations of judges and lawyers, including the largely self-taught Abraham Lincoln, made a similar argument. He asserted that the "law of nature" (a term he and others used because they believed that this higher moral law is part of nature) is "superior in obligation to any other" and that "no human laws are of any validity if contrary to this."[7]

And so, in arguing that we are not bound in conscience to obey unjust laws, King wasn't just spinning something out of thin air.

ARE UNJUST LAWS REALLY LAWS?

But just because a particular view dates back centuries doesn't necessarily mean that it is right. After all, the racism that King was working so hard to end also had a history several centuries old. And so anyone engaging in thoughtful discussion of these matters must ask whether it indeed does makes sense to talk about a higher law that stands in judgment of human law and to assert that unjust laws are not binding on conscience.

The critics of natural law frequently contend that to use a moral screen to determine which laws are valid and which are not would invite chaos. In an era in which there are widely divergent views about matters such as abortion, physician-assisted suicide, and same-sex marriage, it is difficult to dispute this point. Whose moral values should be used to determine which laws are valid and which are not, which laws to enforce and which to set aside? Would it just be "the luck of the draw," with the validity of laws determined by the moral whims of whoever happened to be the presiding judge? These are weighty matters. One can well imagine that chaos would reign supreme if judges attempted to use moral screens to determine which laws should be enforced and which should not.

This point did not escape Blackstone. In an extended footnote commenting on the passage in which he asserted that human laws derive their validity from natural law, he took issue with Lord Chief Justice Hobart, who, according to Blackstone, "has also advanced, that even an act of parliament, made against natural justice . . . is void in itself." Blackstone continued, "With deference to these high authorities, I should conceive that in no case whatever can a judge oppose his own opinion and authority to the clear will and declaration of the legislature." He added, "And if an act of parliament, if we could suppose such a case, should, like the edict of Herod, command all the children under a certain age to be slain, the judge ought to resign his office rather than be auxiliary to its execution." Such a law, however, "could only be declared void by the same legislative body by which it was ordained."[8]

And so Blackstone, in suggesting that laws have to satisfy certain moral criteria in order to be binding on conscience, was not also suggesting that judges should use a moral screen to determine which laws should be enforced. While stopping short of saying that unjust laws ought to be enforced, Blackstone took the position that judges do not have the authority themselves to set aside unjust laws—only Parliament can do that—but instead ought to resign rather than be involved in the enforcement of unjust laws.

WHY, IF AT ALL, SHOULD WE COMPLY WITH THE LAW?

The question of whether judges should use a moral screen to determine which laws to enforce is one matter. The question of why, if at all, we ought to comply with the law (or do anything else) is quite another.

Why should we comply with the law? "Just because it's there" isn't a very good answer. As the segregation laws on the books prior to the civil rights movement serve to remind us, laws might embody all sorts of evil. When King made the distinction between just and unjust laws in his "Letter from Birmingham Jail," he forcefully drove home the point by noting that almost everything the Nazis did in Germany was "legal" in the sense that it was consistent with laws on the books. Nor is it satisfactory to say that we ought to comply with the law "because we'll get in trouble if we don't." If compliance with the law were simply a matter of avoiding penalties, law would be nothing more than an exercise in coercion, and there would be no reason to comply with the law if one believed it possible to avoid the penalties for failure to comply.

The English philosopher John Locke (1632–1704) argued that we ought to obey the law because we have agreed to do so. The practical problem with consent theory, however, is that it is very difficult to point to occasions when promises of this sort have been made (apart from naturalization ceremonies for those not native-born). Locke claimed that we often fail to notice consent because it is given "in a multitude."[9] This, however, doesn't solve the problem, because things done in large groups are still noticeable, particularly if one focuses attention on the particular individuals who make up the groups. For example, when watching a football game, it is possible to overlook what a particular player—say, the left offensive guard or the strong-side safety—does. However, focusing on that player to the exclusion of all other players makes it possible to observe what that player does, even on plays in which he is not directly involved.

Locke also made reference to "tacit consent," which he believed is given by enjoying any of the benefits provided by a government and "reaches as far as the very being of anyone within the territories of that government."[10] However, if one understands consent as something that must be given consciously and freely, consent isn't something that someone can be tricked into giving or something that can be given without the person allegedly doing the consenting being aware of what she or he is doing. It won't do to say to a weary traveler who has just arrived in this country, "Congratulations, you have just promised to obey the laws of the United States of America!" The weary traveler might well be justified in responding, "I have? All that I thought that I was doing was visiting my aunt in Toledo." As the Scottish philosopher David Hume (1711–76) observed with respect to consent theorists, "But would these reasoners look abroad into the world, they would meet with nothing that, in the least, corresponds to their ideas, or can warrant so refined a system."[11]

Moreover, even if consent on the part of all citizens could clearly be identified, this still wouldn't provide a basis for arguing that there is an obligation to comply with the law, since there is still the moral question of why we are obligated to keep our promises, and under what circumstances.[12] As Hume put it, "We are bound to obey our sovereign, it is said, because we have given a tacit promise to that purpose. But why are we bound to observe our promise?"[13] If consent theory ultimately depends on the moral claim that we ought to keep our promises, why not approach the question of obligation directly by asserting on moral grounds that there is an obligation to comply with the law? Consent theory might have played a significant historical role in efforts to secure more democratic forms of government, but as a theory of obligation, it is deficient.

The question remains: why, if at all, should we comply with the law? Augustine told a story about a pirate who was captured and brought before Alexander the Great. The pirate, when asked what he was doing trying to maintain hostile possession of the seas, replied that he and the emperor were really trying to do the same thing. The only difference, the pirate insisted, was that "because I do it with a petty ship, I am called a robber whilst thou who dost it with a great fleet art styled emperor." Commenting on the story, Augustine asked rhetorically, "Indeed, without justice, what are kingdoms but great robberies?"[14]

Augustine was not mistaken. Without justice, government, with its power to tax and coerce, is nothing but robbery on a grand scale. Whatever obligation we might have to comply with the law derives from justice and other moral considerations. And therein lies the dilemma, for in this age of ethical pluralism, we can no longer assume that there is a common core of moral beliefs that provides a basis for arguing that government or anything or anyone else can legitimately be characterized as possessing moral authority. To these matters we now turn.

Ten Questions for Reflection and Discussion

1   Were Martin Luther King Jr. and Thomas Aquinas right in suggesting that there is not an obligation to obey unjust laws?

2   As you see things, under what circumstances, if any, is disobeying the law justifiable?

3   Which standard of morality should be used in determining whether a law is just or unjust?

4   Whose standard of morality should be used?

5   Should unjust laws be enforced?

6   To what extent, if at all, does it make sense to say that all citizens of a particular country such as the United States have agreed to obey the law?

7   Is there such a thing as "tacit consent"? If so, what are its distinguishing features?

8   Was John Locke right in suggesting that anyone who enjoys any of the benefits provided by a government consents to obeying its laws?

9   Why, if at all, should we keep our promises?

10 What types of authority, if any, are identifiable in contemporary society? Why, if at all, should they be viewed as possessing authority?

NOTES

1. For a firsthand account of the events in Birmingham, see "Bull Connor's Birmingham," "New Day in Birmingham," and "Letter from Birmingham Jail," in *Why We Can't Wait,* by Martin Luther King Jr. (New York: Signet Books, 1964), 47–95. For a highly readable biography of King, see Stephen B. Gates, *Let the Trumpet Sound: The Life of Martin Luther King Jr.* (New York: Harper & Row, 1982). His narrative of the events in Birmingham can be found on 209–32.

2. Gates, *Let the Trumpet Sound,* 209.

3. King, "New Day in Birmingham," 70.

4. King, "Letter from Birmingham Jail," 82.

5. Augustine's statement, which in its entirety reads, "For a law that is unjust does not seem to me to be a law at all," is found in his essay "On Free Will," *Augustine: Earlier Writings,* trans. John H. S. Burleigh (Philadelphia: Westminster Press, 1953), 118 (1,5,11).

6. Thomas Aquinas, *Summa Theologica,* trans. Fathers of the English Dominican Province (New York: Benziger, 1947), I-II, Q.96, A.3.

7. Sir William Blackstone, *Commentaries on the Laws of England, Book 1,* 15th ed. (London: A. Strahan, 1809), 40–41.

8. Blackstone, *Commentaries on the Laws of England,* 40–41.

9. John Locke, *The Second Treatise of Government,* ed. Thomas Peardon (Indianapolis: Bobbs-Merrill, 1952), 67 (VIII, 117).

10. Locke, *Second Treatise,* 68 (VIII, 119). See also Thomas Hobbes, *Leviathan: Or the Matter, Forme and Power of a Commonwealth Ecclesticall and Civil,* ed. Michael Oakeshott (New York: Collier Books, 1962). Hobbes speaks of contracts being made "by inference" and states that "generally a sign by inference, of any contract, is whatsoever sufficiently argues the will of the contractor" (106). Fair enough. But even if consent is implied, it must be given consciously and deliberately, which is where the shoe starts pinching when it comes to consent of significance with respect to any obligation we might have to comply with the law.

11. David Hume, "Of the Original Contract," in *Hume: Theory of Politics,* ed. Frederick Watkins (Edinburgh: Thomas Nelson & Sons, 1951), 197.

12. Promises are customarily understood as imposing obligations on the

person making the promise, obligations that person has in addition to whatever other obligations he or she has as a parent, a citizen, a neighbor, or as part of other roles in which he or she might be functioning. Obligations derived from promises, however, make sense only if there indeed is an obligation to keep promises.

13. Hume, "Of the Original Contract," 209.

14. Augustine, *City of God,* IV, 4, in *The Political Writings of St. Augustine,* ed. Henry Paolucci (Chicago: Henry Regnery, 1962), 29–30. The selection is drawn from the translation by George Wilson, who assisted Marcus Dods, the primary translator for the 1872 edition of *City of God.* Paolucci, however, has taken some editorial license with Wilson's translation. Wilson translated the first sentence as "Justice being taken away, then, what are kingdoms but great robberies?" The Paolucci version, cited in the text above, states, "Indeed, without justice, what are kingdoms but great robberies?" The Paolucci version is smoother stylistically but not as faithful to the Latin text, which makes reference to justice being removed: "Remota itaque iustitia quid sunt regna nisi magna latrocinia?"

2

WHAT COUNTS AS JUSTICE?

—

And so the quest for a basis for obligation must move from law to morality. If any obligation to comply with a law derives, at least in part, from its moral content, we must confront head-on the question of what constitutes justice, as well as a host of other moral questions. But, as Shakespeare's Hamlet put it, albeit in a somewhat different context, "Ay, there's the rub,"[1] for in an age of pluralism, there is no universally accepted answer that can be given to moral questions.[2]

In *The Nicomachean Ethics*, Aristotle (384–322 B.C.E.), in the judgment of many the greatest philosopher of all time, speaks of two particular types of justice: distributive justice and corrective justice. Distributive justice "is shown in the distribution of honour or money or such other possessions of the community as can be divided among its members," while corrective justice "is shown in private transactions or business deals, where it serves the purpose of correcting any unfairness that may arise." Aristotle goes on to subdivide corrective justice into two parts: "voluntary transactions" and "involuntary transactions." The first part includes "buying, selling, loaning money at interest or without interest, pledging, depositing, hiring out"—issues of justice that today are often addressed in civil law. The second deals with crimes such as theft, killing, perjury, and assault and battery—issues of justice that today are addressed in criminal law.[3]

Aristotle's typology is helpful in sorting out the various aspects of justice. However, in the pluralistic society in which we live, it does not resolve the question of what counts as justice. Take, for example, the matter of distributive justice. Aristotle suggests that merit should play a role in determining who should get how much.[4] And indeed, in certain situations, merit criteria do play a role in allocation decisions—for example, year-end productivity bonuses and salary increases (though there are often some who believe that salary increases ought to be across the board, rather than based on merit). In other situations, such as allocation of organs available for transplant, there are strong voices calling for distribution based on need, with some type of random choice such as first-come, first-served determining who among those with similar needs should receive the organ, with no consideration given to merit.[5] In still other cases, there are strong voices insisting that allocation of scarce resources be made in a utilitarian manner that will best serve society—on the basis of potential future contributions, rather than on the basis of past accomplishments.

A historical example illustrates this point. During the Allied campaign in North Africa in 1943, penicillin was in short supply. The U.S. Army theater medical commander had to decide between allocating the available penicillin to (a) soldiers wounded in combat whose wounds were infected and (b) soldiers who had been, as one commentator put it, "wounded in brothels"—that is, those with venereal disease.[6] Both conditions could be treated successfully with what was known as "the miracle drug" in the days before antibiotic-resistant strains of bacteria made their presence known. There wasn't enough penicillin, however, to treat both groups of soldiers. If Aristotle had been there, the soldiers wounded in action would undoubtedly have gotten the penicillin, since they were presumably more deserving than those of their comrades incapacitated as a result of sexual escapades in houses of prostitution.

Aristotle, however, didn't happen to be the U.S. Army theater medical commander, and so merit criteria for distribution did not come into play. Instead, the penicillin went to those "wounded in brothels" because it was determined that they would recover more rapidly than those wounded in action and, accordingly, could be sent back into battle sooner than those with infected wounds.[7] And so it was that those wounded in action got Purple Hearts and letters expressing the gratitude of the nation but no penicillin, while those who had picked up venereal disease while fooling around in houses of prostitution got penicillin but no letters of gratitude.

I shall leave to other occasions more detailed discussion of the ethics of the U.S. Army theater medical commander's 1943 decision, as well other more particular issues of distributive justice. Suffice it to say that in the pluralistic society in which we live, there are sharply differing views as to how money and other scarce resources ought to be allocated—or, if one looks at the other side of the coin, how costs ought to be allocated. The same is true with respect to many other issues of justice, as reflected in both civil law and criminal law. For example, the clash between private property rights and the need to build roads, airports, and other things that serve the common good is a hot-button issue in western states and many other parts of the country.[8] Similarly, there is heated debate as to whether *Roe v. Wade*, the U.S. Supreme Court decision that legalized abortion during the first two-thirds of pregnancy, serves the cause of justice.[9] Many who believe that human life begins at the time of conception view *Roe v. Wade* as having legalized murder, while many feminists and others who place strong emphasis on the rights of women view the controversial decision as justice that was long overdue.[10] Finally, as the intense controversy about capital punishment illustrates, even when there is agreement that certain things ought not be done—for example, killing other people in cold blood—there is no consensus as to what type of punishment best serves the cause of justice.

TWO APPROACHES TO ETHICAL DECISION MAKING

In large part, where one comes out on capital punishment and a host of other controversial issues depends on how one goes about making moral judgments—in short, the style of ethical decision making that one employs. (I am here using the terms "moral" and "ethical" inter-changeably; while some philosophers and theologians make a distinction between moral and ethical judgments, I do not find the distinction particularly useful in most situations.)[11] Sketched in somewhat general terms, there are two basic approaches to ethical decision making. *Deontological* approaches (the term comes from the Greek word for duty) suggest that we have duties to act in certain ways. In contrast, *consequentialist* approaches suggest that the consequences of an act determine its morality.[12] If the good consequences outweigh the bad consequences, it's the right thing to do. If the bad consequences outweigh the good consequences, it's the wrong thing to do.[13]

Two examples serve to illustrate the differences between deontological and consequentialist approaches to ethics. In an essay entitled "On a Supposed Right to Lie from Altruistic Motives," Immanuel Kant (1724–1804), the distinguished German philosopher of the Age of Enlightenment, addresses the question of whether one could in good conscience lie to a murderer pursuing a friend to whom one has given refuge. Kant assumes that when asked about the whereabouts of the friend to whom refuge has been given, it is not possible to avoid answering yes or no. Could one in good conscience lie to the murderer in order to protect the friend? Not according to Kant. He comments, "Each man has not only a right but even the strict duty to be truthful in statements he cannot avoid making, whether they harm himself or others."[14]

Most folks today don't find Kant's truth-telling argument very compelling, preferring a consequentialist approach in this type of situation. "Don't get hung up on literally sticking to telling the truth," they would advise. "Do whatever is likely to work out best in this situation. If resorting to deception offers the best chance of protecting your friend from the murderer, lie with every bit of skill you can muster in the hope that the murderer will go elsewhere, rather than discover the friend to whom you have given refuge." If only the example cited by Kant were noted, many would undoubtedly wonder why anyone would want to be anything other than a consequentialist.

Consider, however, a very different case. In the late 1950s, the *New England Journal of Medicine* reported a series of experiments conducted on residents of the Willowbrook State School, a home for mentally handicapped children located on Staten Island in New York. The experiments were directed toward determining whether injections of gamma globulin would reduce the incidence of infectious hepatitis. Researchers chose Willowbrook as the site of the experiments because there was already a low-grade epidemic of hepatitis there. In the early rounds of the experiments, researchers gave gamma globulin to some of the children and compared the results with those of children who had not received gamma globulin. As the experiments continued, newly admitted children and the group of children who had not received gamma globulin were divided into two groups, with one group receiving gamma globulin and the other group serving as a control group. Even though many staff members had been exposed to hepatitis, they were not used as subjects for the experiments.[15]

In the early 1960s, Willowbrook was closed to new admissions because of overcrowding. The administrators of the home, however, made exceptions for children whose parents were willing to allow them to be involved in the hepatitis study—that is, children whose parents were willing to allow them to be exposed to hepatitis as part of the study. In some variations of the experiments, children who had been inoculated with gamma globulin were fed the hepatitis virus, obtained from the feces of other children, to see if gamma globulin would protect them from the virus.[16]

The experiments were successful. They had a good outcome. The good consequences outweighed the bad. But does that justify them? In *The Patient as Person*, a groundbreaking book in the field of medical ethics, theologian Paul Ramsey (1913–88) sharply criticizes the Willowbrook experiments, notwithstanding the fact that they were successful. He insists that "children in institutions and not directly under the care of parents or relatives should *never* be used in medical investigations having present pain or discomfort and unknown present and future risks to them, and promising future possible benefits only for others."[17]

RULE DEONTOLOGY

When a lot of folks think about ethics, one of the first things to come to mind is a rule. Sometimes a lot of rules. And indeed, many approaches to ethics do involve rules, ranging from the first time our parents "laid down the law" to us when we were children to elaborate codes of conduct intended to ensure high ethical standards in the business world or elsewhere.[18] Sometimes rules are carefully codified and published in the form of laws and institutional policies. In other cases, they are unwritten guides to conduct. Sometimes rules are articulated by distinguished scholars such as Kant, whose categorical imperative—"Act only in accordance with that maxim through which you can at the same time will that it should become a universal law"—is a frequent reference point for discussions of ethics.[19] In other cases, they have a far less illustrious lineage, having been crafted by persons unknown or once known but now forgotten. Sometimes, as in the case of the Ten Commandments or the teachings of the Qur'an, they are part of centuries-old religious traditions. In other cases, they are drafted to respond to particular situations. Sometimes rules prohibit certain types of conduct—for example, "You shall not steal" (Exodus

20.15).[23] In other cases, they prescribe specified courses of action—for example, "Remember the sabbath day, and keep it holy" (Exodus 20.8). But whether new or old, of distinguished lineage or of unknown origin, negative or positive, all rules have the following characteristic: they are generalized value statements about specified categories or classes of acts.

The rule approach to ethical decision making, it should be noted, is simply a way of making ethical decisions. There are many different sets of rules, some of them completely at odds with other sets of rules. To illustrate this point to a class I was teaching, I once observed that even the Mafia has a code of conduct, though, I added, presumably not the same code of conduct as any of those held by members of the class. A student stopped by after class and remarked, "I sure was happy to hear you mention the Mafia. I can really identify with that! Both my mother and father come from Mafia families." I chose not to pursue the matter.

The way that the content of rules varies can be illustrated by looking at the way that institutional rules have changed in the course of the years. Take, for example, rules on smoking. In years gone by, smoking was completely prohibited at a number of colleges and universities, including the college where I have taught for nearly three decades. But then the rules were relaxed a bit, first with respect to men and then, as the equal rights movement changed the way that many people viewed things, with respect to women as well. In the late 1960s and early 1970s, there were few, if any, rules about smoking at many colleges and universities. Both as an undergraduate and as a graduate student, I was enrolled in classes in which students and professors alike lit up cigars and pipes and filled the room with an impenetrable blue haze. (And yes, though I quit smoking several years ago when my then ten-year-old daughter had a little talk with me about the evils of smoking, I must confess that as a student I was among those who detracted from the air quality of many classrooms.) But then, the rules once again changed.

At the college where I teach, the new rules on smoking initially prohibited smoking in classrooms and in dining halls. Then the rules were expanded to include lounges, faculty offices, and wings of residence halls that were declared "smoke-free." In time, rules prohibiting smoking were extended to all buildings on campus. What a difference a few decades make!

POSITIVE AND NEGATIVE RIGHTS

This is an appropriate place to comment on two very different notions of rights, notions that interface with the two types of rules (positive rules that say "Thou shalt" and negative rules that say "Thou shalt not"). Positive rights, sometimes referred to as rights of entitlement, assert that something is owed to the bearer of the right—that is, that he or she is entitled to receive something. For example, someone who works in a school cafeteria is entitled to receive a paycheck, in keeping with the terms of employment.[21] Note also that if this employee is to receive a paycheck, someone—often the payroll clerk—has to do something, that is, cut the check and make certain that it is sent to the employee. In short, there is a "thou shalt" rule addressed to the payroll clerk that specifies what must be done in order to make good on the cafeteria worker's right to compensation.

It might be added that it makes little sense to talk about rights of entitlement without going on to address the question of whose job it is to make good on the right in question. For example, in any number of discussions there are those who speak of a "right to basic health care," which in any society committed to human decency is a noble sentiment indeed. But if asked whose job it is to make good on this right of entitlement, it is not unusual for those asserting that there is a right to basic health care to respond by saying, "It's society's responsibility" (whoever "society" might be). Or sometimes they respond by simply saying,

"Something ought to be done about that." That's not good enough. If we are to be serious about basic health care as a right of entitlement, it is essential that we address the twin questions of how it will be funded and what type of health care delivery system is necessary in order to ensure universal access to basic health care.

In contrast to positive rights, negative rights, sometimes also called rights of forbearance, are respected when other people stay out of the way and refrain from interfering.[22] Take, for example, a right of privacy. How is someone's right of privacy respected? By other people refraining from snooping around where they have no business snooping around, peering through windows that they have no business peering through, reading confidential files that they have no business reading, etc. The same is true of all other negative rights. In effect, there is an accompanying negative rule directed toward others that says, "Thou shalt not."

Most of the basic freedoms that are part of our political traditions are negative rights. For example, you have freedom of speech if—and only if—others refrain from doing bad things to you when you speak your mind. If you are in danger of getting fired if you tell you boss to his face what you think of his new toupee, you don't have freedom of speech.[23] Colleges and university faculty members have academic freedom only if their jobs aren't at risk if they give expression to controversial views. Students have academic freedom only if they do not risk receiving a lower grade if they disagree with the instructor. Similarly, we have freedom of religion only if others refrain from persecuting us if we practice what they view as the wrong brand of religion—or no religion at all. We have freedom of assembly only if others refrain from disrupting our meetings when we assemble. The common theme in all of this is that we have freedoms of the sorts just noted only if others refrain from intervening—that is, exercise restraint or forbearance.

Though the significance of the distinction between positive and negative rights is often overlooked, it plays a role in the lines that the U.S.

Supreme Court has drawn with respect to abortion. In *Roe v. Wade*, the pivotal 1973 decision that substantially redefined the legal landscape with respect to abortion, the Supreme Court ruled that states cannot prohibit abortion prior to the time of viability (the time that the fetus can survive outside the womb, should birth occur). In effect, the Court ruled that pregnant women have negative rights—that is, rights of non-interference—with respect to abortion, at least prior to the time of viability. What many have failed to note, however, is that the Supreme Court has never ruled that women have constitutionally mandated positive rights—that is, rights of entitlement—with respect to abortion.[24] In *Harris v. McRae* and *Webster v. Reproductive Health Services*, which have sometimes mistakenly been interpreted as scaling back abortion rights, the Court ruled that states may limit funding for abortion and prohibit the use of government facilities for abortion.[25] However, the major tenet of *Roe v. Wade*—the ruling that abortion may not be prohibited during the first two-thirds of the pregnancy—remains unchanged.

COMMAND DEONTOLOGY

While the rule approach to ethics is probably the most prevalent deontological approach, it is by no means the only one. The command model has also played a prominent role, both historically and in contemporary society.

Sometimes the command model is set in a theological framework, with God viewed as the command giver. For example, in *Church Dogmatics*, twentieth-century Swiss theologian Karl Barth (1886–1968) argues that God "gives us His command. . . . The question cannot be whether he speaks, but only whether we hear."[26] In other cases, which are somewhat more common today, the command model is placed in a social setting in which specified individuals are viewed as authoritative command givers. For example, the military has a very clearly defined command and control system. Everyone, up to and including the chair of the Joint Chiefs of Staff, has a commanding officer and is expected to take very seriously whatever orders are issued by that commanding officer. A traditional view of the role of physicians in relation to other health care professionals, which is now being replaced by a more collegial model, holds that physicians are authority figures who give orders and it is the job of other health care professionals to comply with these orders. In most business organizations, there is the expectation that if your boss tells you to do something, you ought to do what your boss tells you to do.

The command model does insist that if there is any question about the authenticity of the orders, it is important to make certain that they were issued by a legitimate source of authority. During the Battle of the Bulge in December of 1944, English-speaking German soldiers put on captured U.S. uniforms, infiltrated American lines, and disrupted things as much as possible by issuing bogus orders, changing road signs, and spreading false rumors.[27] But be it on the battlefield or elsewhere, once authenticity is verified, the command model expects those receiving the orders to do whatever they are ordered to do—tell the truth, falsify records, give money to charity, kill someone, or do anything else that they might be ordered to do.

A sad and tragic story illustrates this point. A few years ago at a reception celebrating the centennial of a school of nursing in our area, I had occasion to visit with a retired nurse who at that time must have been in her late seventies or early eighties. Early in her career, she had worked in the delivery room at one of the area hospitals helping obstetricians deliver babies. One obstetrician, whom she did not name, took it upon himself to make certain that any newborn infant with major birth defects did not survive. The delivery room was located on one of the upper floors of the hospital with a window overlooking the roof of a lower level. On a bitterly cold winter day, the obstetrician ordered the nurse to open the window and place on the roof a newborn infant with birth defects until she stopped crying. The nurse did what she was told to do and has been forever haunted by the memory of that terrible day. Regulations that are now in place would prevent from happening today what happened on that cold winter day more than a half century ago. But they came far too late to be of any help to the nurse haunted by the memory of what she did.[28]

CONSEQUENTIALISM: A RESULTS-ORIENTED APPROACH

When making ethical decisions, rule deontologists begin by asking, "What do the rules say?" Command deontologists ask, "What does my boss want me to do?" Consequentialists come at the matter from an entirely different direction. They begin by asking, "What's likely to happen?" Consequentialism is a results-oriented approach. Securing the best possible outcome is what consequentialism is all about.

For the consequentialist, it's the future that counts. If choosing between giving a liver available for transplant to a sixty-three-year-old retired physician or a twenty-three-year-old medical student with a promising future ahead of her if she can regain her health, the consequentialist would give the liver to the medical student. The past is of significance to the consequentialist only insofar as it provides a data bank for making projections about the future. Rather ironically, the long records of distinguished service by the sixty-three-year-old retired physician and other physicians provide the data that consequentialists use to predict that the medical student will help many in the future if she can regain her health and complete medical school.

Consequentialism by its very nature demands that we speculate about the future, which, by definition, is very difficult to study. Sometimes, drawing upon years of experience or theoretical knowledge, we make predictions with a high degree of confidence. Suppose that some-one holds a book at arm's length and predicts that when he or she lets go of it, it will fall to the floor rather than fly up and stick to the ceiling. The odds are pretty good that's what will happen, barring unforeseen circumstances such as an earthquake that turns the room upside down.

In other cases, we have no clear sense of the consequences that might result from whatever is being contemplated. For example, will preim-plantation genetic diagnosis (screening pre-embryos for in vitro fertil-ization in a laboratory to determine which should be implanted) adversely affect the nature of the parent-child relationship? If preim-plantation genetic diagnosis becomes common practice, will children who are born with birth defects suffer from discrimination? Will they have psychological problems, feeling that they have been cheated out of good health by the failure of their parents to practice preimplantation genetic screening? And if preimplantation genetic diagnosis is used to prevent the transmission of debilitating diseases, is it simply a matter of time until the technique is used to select characteristics that are viewed as desirable, such as eye color, perfect pitch, and athletic ability? No one knows the answers to these questions.

The fact that we don't always know what is going to happen, howev-er, doesn't mean that we should ignore potential consequences when making ethical decisions. Indeed, many would argue that if we are to be responsible decision makers, it is incumbent upon us to consider poten-tial consequences. On one occasion while in college, I hitched a ride with a college classmate who was driving to Minneapolis. As we were traveling along an interstate highway at a high rate of speed, the front end of the car began vibrating and shaking in a rather disconcerting manner. I glanced at the speedometer. The needle was hovering in the vicinity of 125 miles per hour. My friend, attempting to reassure me, said "Don't worry. The speedometer's wrong. We're only going 120."

Because of the risk factors, driving down the highway at 120 miles per hour is not, in the judgment of those concerned about preventing death and injury, a very smart thing to do. Granted, no one knows for certain what will happen. As in the case of my friend, a recklessly speeding motorist might reach his or her destination in record time. However, it is also possible that a serious accident will result, causing death and grave injury. (By the way, I discovered that my schedule did not allow me to join my friend for the return trip.)

WHAT COUNTS AS A GOOD CONSEQUENCE? (AND WHAT COUNTS AS A BAD CONSEQUENCE?)

Trying to anticipate what might happen is only the first step in any consequentialist approach to ethical decision making. The second step is evaluating the expected consequences in order to determine whether the good consequences outweigh the bad consequences. In order to do this, it is necessary to identify the criteria to be used in assessing the consequences—value yardsticks that might be used to sort out the good consequences from the bad consequences and to determine how good or how bad the consequences might be.

In some cases, there is rough agreement as to what is likely to happen if a particular course of action is taken. Take, for example, the question of whether old-growth forest that is the habitat for the spotted owl should be logged, a matter of considerable controversy in recent years. A certain number of people on both sides of the debate pretty much agree on what is likely to happen if old-growth forest is cut down for lumber. Jobs will be generated in the timber industry. High-quality lumber will be made available at a lower cost than that made from less desirable timber. The habitat for the spotted owl will be diminished, perhaps pushing it to the brink of distinction. The old-growth forest will be gone forever.

Just mapping out what is likely to happen, however, doesn't resolve the question of whether logging old-growth forest is a good or bad thing to do. Those who are pro-logging tend to emphasize the economic advantages of harvesting the trees while downplaying the significance of the environmental impact. In contrast, environmentalists tend to attach far higher significance to environmental preservation than do those who favor logging.[29] Therein lies the nub of the controversy. In like manner, differing views about how consequences should be assessed account for much of the disagreement about other, controversial matters.

CONSEQUENCES FOR WHOM?

Sorting out the criteria to be used in assessing consequences is an important step along the way when making consequentialist judgments. But there's still more to be done. Either explicitly or implicitly, the consequentialist must decide what range of consequences to take into consideration when making consequentialist decisions.

A consequence isn't something suspended in thin air. It is something that happens to someone. Take, for example, the matter of profits and losses, which are types of consequences. Suppose that someone were to say with respect to a particular housing development, "There sure was a bundle of money made on that project!" but when asked who made the money responded by saying, "No one made any money; it was just made." That wouldn't make any sense at all. If money was made on the project, it had to show up on someone's balance sheet. Ditto for losses.

The same is true for all consequences. One way or other, they show up on someone's balance sheet. (I am here using the term somewhat broadly to encompass all gains or losses, not just financial gains or losses.) A crucial question for the consequentialist, however, is the following: whose balance sheet(s) should be considered when deciding whether the good consequences outweigh the bad consequences? Just your own balance sheet? The balance sheets of everyone who might be affected by the act in question? The balance sheets of a more limited group—that is, some but not all? These are tremendously important questions insofar as consequentialism is concerned.

INDIVIDUAL CONSEQUENTIALISM

The most limited form of consequentialism is individual consequentialism, which focuses exclusively on the balance sheet of one individual, ignoring the impact on anyone else. That individual might be yourself or someone else. If the individual is yourself, you essentially will operate on the basis of self-interest, doing whatever is to your own advantage even if others are harmed by what you do. This approach, which is certainly not unknown in the history of humankind, is sometimes referred to as *ethical egoism*.[30]

Examples of individual consequentialism in which the beneficiary is someone other than the individual making the decision are a little more difficult to identify. Consider, however, the following. Suppose that your fourteen-year-old cousin inherits $14 million and you are named as the trustee for the trust fund in which the $14 million is parked. In keeping with the notion of fiduciary responsibility, you would be expected to manage that trust fund exclusively with the best interests of your cousin in mind. You wouldn't be allowed to skim off a couple of million dollars for yourself. You couldn't even give any of the money to charity unless you could prove that doing so would benefit your cousin to a greater extent than leaving the money in the trust fund and investing it prudently. In short, in this scenario, there is only one balance sheet to be considered: that of your cousin.

Other examples of individual consequentialism focusing on the balance sheet of someone other than the decision maker include a very traditional view of the doctor-patient relationship—the old "doctor knows best" approach. This view holds that (a) the doctor is the decision maker, and (b) the doctor should focus exclusively on what's best for the patient. Another example is provided by a traditional understanding of the lawyer-client relationship that holds that it is the job of a defense attorney to secure the best possible outcome for his or her client.[31]

GROUP CONSEQUENTIALISM

There isn't anything particularly profound about the notion of group consequentialism. It is something more than individual consequentialism, which considers the balance sheet of just one individual, and something less than ethical universalism, which considers the balance sheets of everyone who might be affected by the act in question. If the trust fund for which you are the trustee is inherited by three of your cousins, rather than just one, your responsibilities, as defined by the notion of fiduciary responsibility, fall in the realm of group consequentialism rather than individual consequentialism. If you advocate some form of nationalism—that is, argue that we ought to act on the basis of national self-interest, even if what is done might not be advantageous to people living in other countries—you are a group consequentialist. If you are part of an advocacy group lobbying for better treatment for those who are handicapped or those with a particular type of illness, you are a group consequentialist. You might be part of the group for which you are lobbying, or you might be an outside representative speaking on its behalf. But either way, you are a group consequentialist.

UTILITARIANISM

Utilitarianism is the best-known form of ethical universalism. Popularized by two British philosophers, Jeremy Bentham (1748–1832) and

John Stuart Mill (1806–73), utilitarianism advocates doing whatever is in the service or utility of society as a whole—hence the term "utilitarianism." The central tenets of utilitarianism are often summarized as "the greatest good for the greatest number."[32]

Bentham proposed using pleasure and pain as the measure of good and bad consequences, respectively, an approach often referred to as the *hedonistic calculus.* (The label is derived from the Greek word for pleasure.) In a frequently quoted passage, he states, "Nature has placed mankind under the governance of two sovereign masters, *pain* and *pleasure.* It is for them alone to point out what we ought to do, as well as to determine what we shall do."[33]

Believing that the hedonistic calculus placed too much emphasis on bodily pleasure, Mill argued that whatever contributes to happiness should be viewed as good while that which detracts from happiness ought to be viewed as bad. In *Utilitarianism,* one of his best-known works, he asserts, "The creed which accepts as the foundation of morals, Utility, or the Greatest Happiness Principle, holds that actions are right in proportion as they tend to promote happiness, wrong as they tend to produce the reverse of happiness."[34] This variation became known as *eudaimonistic utilitarianism,* the label coming from the Greek word for happiness.

A distinction is sometimes made between *act utilitarianism* and *rule utilitarianism.*[35] When contemplating a particular course of action, the act utilitarian asks, "What is likely to happen if I do this particular act on this particular occasion?" In contrast, the rule utilitarian asks, "What is likely to happen if everyone were to do what I am contemplating doing?" The two questions can lead to very different conclusions. Suppose, for example, that a faculty member late for class contemplates cutting across the lawn between the parking lot and the building in which the classroom is located. If he or she is an act utilitarian, he or she will probably decide that cutting across the lawn on that one occasion won't do any significant damage to the grass and will have the salutary effect of saving a minute or two. On the other hand, a rule utilitarian might well conclude that if everyone late for class were to cut across the lawn between the parking lot and the classroom building, the grass would be destroyed, resulting in a muddy path that would detract from the aesthetic quality of the campus. (The substantial number of muddy paths on the campuses of colleges and universities might suggest that there are more act utilitarians than rule utilitarians at many institutions of higher education.)

SITUATION ETHICS

Situation ethics, a highly flexible approach to ethical decision making popularized by theologian Joseph Fletcher (1905–91), is very similar to utilitarianism. Indeed, Fletcher states that situationism "must form a coalition with utilitarianism" and "[take] over from Bentham and Mill the strategic principle of 'the greatest good of the greatest number.'" The major difference between utilitarianism and situationism, Fletcher suggests, is that situationism should be guided by the Christian notion of love for neighbor—the type of love denoted by the Greek word *agape*. Fletcher suggests that when situationism is combined with utilitarianism, "the hedonistic calculus becomes the agapeic calculus, the greatest amount of neighbor welfare for the largest number of neighbors possible."[36]

Like all forms of consequentialism, including utilitarianism, situationism allows sacrificing individuals if the greater good would be served. Fletcher cites the example of two groups of settlers pursued by war parties as they traveled along the Wilderness Road stretching westward through the Cumberland Gap to Kentucky during the eighteenth century. Both groups sought cover in the hope of escaping detection. In both groups, there was a small baby who, frightened by what was happening, cried out. One woman clung to her crying baby. The mother and baby, along with her other three children and other members of the party, were discovered and killed. The mother in the other group, realizing that her crying child endangered the entire party, killed her child while trying to stifle her crying so that they could maintain silence and safely reach the fort. They did. Though Fletcher concludes the discussion with a rhetorical question, he clearly believes that the woman who sacrificed the life of her child made the right decision by sacrificing one life so that a greater number of lives could be saved.[37]

ANALYTICAL TOOLS

Apart from philosophers and theologians who write papers for professional association meetings, very few people consciously think in the various categories outlined above. I have never been at a party at which someone came up and said, "Hi. I'm an act utilitarian. What are you?" The various models for ethical decision making outlined in the preceding pages, however, provide useful analytical tools for sorting out the ways that we and others make ethical decisions. Though most of us don't consciously think in terms of these categories, if we look at the value judgments that we make about human conduct, we will see various of these approaches reflected in the way that we go about making these value judgments. The same is true with respect to the value judgments made by others.

HYBRID MODELS

Relatively few people are single-model ethical decision makers. Many draw upon various approaches, depending on the situation or the particular issue being addressed. There are many hybrid models that combine elements of more than one approach to ethical decision making.

For example, the command model is often combined with limiting rules that place certain things out of bounds. While military law, as defined by the Uniform Code of Military Justice, strongly emphasizes the importance of following orders, it also notes that they must be lawful orders, thereby placing out of bounds orders such as massacring civilians that are not viewed as lawful.[38] Similarly, laws and regulations, such as the Baby Doe regulations that mandate treatment for most handicapped newborn infants, place limits on what physicians can order those working for them to do.[39]

TWO LEVELS OF ETHICAL DECISION MAKING

As if all of this were not complicated enough, it also bears noting that there are often two distinctly different levels to the ethical decision making process. The first level involves identifying *prima facie obligations*. (The term "prima facie" literally means "first look" or "first glance.") How one goes about identifying prima facie obligations depends upon the style of ethical decision maker that one is—rule deontologist, utilitarian, etc.[40]

If all of our prima facie obligations fit together, they are also our actual obligations. If this is the case, we have come to the end of the ethical decision making process. The only question that remains is whether we have the willpower to make good on our obligations.

In many situations, however, we find that we are pulled in different directions by competing prima facie obligations. In some cases, we can eliminate the conflict by rescheduling one of the tasks that we find that we are obligated to do—for example, find a different time to help a friend move a piece of furniture so that we can remain with a family member who is ill. But in other cases, rescheduling cannot eliminate the conflict. Suppose, for example, that you are taking a critically ill family member to the hospital and encounter a traffic light that is red at 3:15 A.M., with no traffic in sight. Do you make good on your prima facie obligation to get your critically ill family member to the hospital as quickly as possible or make good on your prima facie obligation to comply with traffic laws? At this point the decision-making process gets kicked upstairs to a second level as you decide (rather quickly in this case) which of your competing prima facie obligations takes priority and, hence, is your actual obligation in this particular situation.

If, as most would probably do, you choose to ignore the red light and drive on through the intersection, you would have, in effect, decided that your obligation to get your critically ill family member to the hospital as quickly as possible was the stronger obligation in this particular situation. Note, however, that if you decide to drive on through the intersection in this situation, you are not by implication saying that you have no obligation to comply with traffic laws. You are merely saying that your obligation to get your critically ill family member to the hospital is stronger than your obligation to comply with traffic laws in this particular situation.

With this in mind, let's return to the case about truth telling that Kant addresses in his essay entitled "On the Supposed Right to Lie from Altruistic Motives." Rule deontologists with a rule that says it is wrong to tell a lie do have a way of dealing with this situation without standing at the door and saying to the murderer, "I cannot tell a lie. My friend is hiding in the basement." It is entirely plausible to argue that in this sort of situation there is both a prima facie obligation to tell the truth and a prima facie obligation to protect the friend, with the obligation to protect the friend being the stronger obligation. Just as in the case of driving through a red light while taking a critically ill family member to the hospital, this is in no way to suggest that there is no obligation to tell the truth. It is only to suggest that when the obligation to tell the truth conflicts with the obligation to protect a friend from grave harm, the obligation to protect the friend takes priority.

Finally, it is worth underscoring that when the ethical decision making process gets kicked upstairs and we are forced to choose from among competing prima facie obligations, in a very real sense what we must do is decide which of the things that we ought to do must be left undone. Should we go to that meeting that the boss has asked us to attend or should we go to a high school band concert in which a son or daughter is playing? Should we go home to help a family member celebrate an important anniversary or should we remain on campus to study for final exams? Should we spend spring break with a grandparent who has suffered the loss of a spouse or should we join a group of volunteers going to Appalachia to help build decent housing for low-income families? These are not easy matters to decide. And, human nature being what it is, whatever is left undone often causes pangs of guilt, notwithstanding the fact that it is not humanly possible to do everything that we believe we ought to do.

THE QUESTION OF JUSTICE REVISITED

It is time to return to the question posed at the beginning of this chapter: what counts as justice? In the pluralistic society in which we live, the answer that one gives to this question and other questions of moral significance depends on the approach to ethical decision making that one takes and on the particular values incorporated in this approach. Rule deontologists of various persuasions, command deontologists, utilitarians, situation ethicists, and others are likely to give very different answers to these questions.

Is it possible to single out one set of values as given expression in one particular approach to ethical decision making and conclusively argue that this is the way that questions of justice and other ethical questions ought to be approached? This question forms the agenda for the next chapter.

Ten Questions for Reflection and Discussion

1 As you see things, how should justice be defined?

2 What type(s) of criteria should be used when making allocation decisions?

3 As you see things, to what extent, if at all, is one obligated to tell the truth to the murderer in the case Immanuel Kant discusses?

4 What are your views about the ethics of the Willowbrook experiments?

5 What are the strengths, if any, of rule deontological approaches to ethics? And what are the weaknesses, if any, of this approach?

6 Under what circumstances, if any, do you believe that it is ethically acceptable to disobey orders?

7 What, if anything, is wrong with basing ethical decisions exclusively on self-interest?

8 As you see things, what types of criteria should be used in assessing consequences?

9 What are the strengths, if any, of utilitarianism? And what are the weaknesses, if any?

10 Under what circumstances, if any, do you believe that it is appropriate to sacrifice individuals in order to serve what is perceived to be the greater good?

NOTES

1. William Shakespeare, *Hamlet Prince of Denmark*, ed. Robert Hapsgood (Cambridge: Cambridge University Press, 1999), 177–79 (3.1.56–69). The full passage, which has been memorized by schoolchildren for generations, is as follows:

> To be, or not to be, that is the question—
> Whether 'tis nobler in the mind to suffer
> The slings and arrows of outrageous fortune,
> Or to take arms against a sea of troubles,
> And by opposing end them. To die, to sleep—
> To sleep, perchance to dream. Ay, there's the rub,
> For in that sleep of death what dreams may come,
> When we have shuffled off this mortal coil,
> Must give us pause.

2. In the fourth edition of *Business Ethics* (Englewood Cliffs, N.J.: Prentice Hall, 1995), Richard T. DeGeorge contrasts *radical moral pluralism* with *pluralism of moral principles.* He defines radical moral pluralism as "that state of affairs in which people hold mutually irreconcilable views about morality, such as what the terms *right* and *wrong* mean, and which actions are right or wrong." Unlike pluralism of moral principles, radical moral pluralism stands in the way of constructing a society. As for pluralism of moral principles, he observes:

> Pluralism on the level of moral principles is compatible with social agreement on the morality of many basic practices. Such agreement does not necessarily involve agreement on the moral principles that different people use to evaluate practices. The vast majority of the members of our society, for instance, agree that murder is wrong. Some members of our society operate only at the level of conventional morality and do not ask why murder is wrong. Some may believe it is wrong because the God in whom they believe forbids such acts; others because it violates human dignity; still others because murder has serious consequences for society as a whole; and so on. (47–48)

The type of pluralism to which reference is here being made is more close-ly akin to what DeGeorge labels pluralism of moral principles than to radical moral pluralism, though the latter is undoubtedly also present in contempo-rary American society in some cases.

3. Aristotle, *The Nicomachean Ethics*, trans. H. Rackham and J. A. K. Thomson (Baltimore: Penguin Books, 1953), 144–45 (V, 2).

4. Aristotle, *Nichomachean Ethics*, 145–46 (V, 3).

5. See, e.g., James F. Childress, "Who Shall Live When Not All Can Live?" in *Bioethics*, ed. Thomas A. Shannon, rev. ed. (Ramsey, N.J.: Paulist Press, 1981), 501–15; and Paul Ramsey, *The Patient as Person* (New Haven: Yale University Press, 1970), 256.

6. Ramsey, *Patient as Person*, 257.

7. Ramsey, *Patient as Person*, 257.

8 See, e.g., Larry Salzman, "New Eminent Domain Assaults: Taking Pri-vate Property for Political Elite," www.aynrand.org/medialink/eminent.shtml [accessed 5 October 2001]. For a more balanced discussion of the issue, see Richard A. Epstein, *Takings: Private Property and the Power of Eminent Domain* (Cambridge: Harvard University Press, 1985). He states, "My thesis is that the eminent domain approach, as applied both to personal liberty and private property, offers a principled account of both the functions of the state and the limitations upon its powers" (331). He concludes, "It is possible, both as a matter of constitutional law and political theory, to articulate common con-ceptions of right and wrong to resolve disputes that individuals have with each other and with the state. These principles do not rest upon any single value but seek to merge the three dominant strands of thought—libertarian, utilitarian, and even redistributive—into a coherent theory of individual rights and polit-ical obligations" (349).

9. *Roe v. Wade*, 410 U.S. 113 (1973). The decision states, "If the State is interested in protecting fetal life after viability, it may go so far as to proscribe abortion during that period except when it is necessary to preserve the life or health of the mother." Though there is considerable debate as to when viabil-ity is first present, the Supreme Court has operated on the assumption that viability is not possible prior to the twenty-fourth week of pregnancy.

10. See, e.g., Pope John Paul II, "The Unspeakable Crime of Abortion," Mary Anne Warren, "On the Moral and Legal Status of Abortion," Don Mar-quis, "Why Abortion Is Immoral," Judith Jarvis Thomson, "A Defense of

Abortion," Daniel Callahan, "Abortion Decisions: Personal Morality," and Susan Sherwin, "The Politics of Abortion," in *Biomedical Ethics*, ed. Thomas A. Mappes and David DeGrazia, 5th ed. (Boston: McGraw Hill, 2001), 454–76, 488–90; Rebecca S. Dresser, "Freedom of Conscience, Professional Responsibility, and Access to Abortion," Mary Anne Warren, "The Moral Significance of Birth," and Laura Purdy, "Abortion, Forced Labor, and War," in *Bioethics, Justice, and Health Care*, ed. Wanda Teays and Laura M. Purdy (Belmont, Calif.: Wadsworth/Thomson Learning, 2001), 464–72, 477–88; and Beverly Wilding Harrison with Shirley Cloyes, "Theology and the Morality of Procreative Choice," and Sidney Callahan, "Abortion and the Sexual Agenda," in *Moral Issues and Christian Response*, ed. Paul T. Jersild, Dale A. Johnson, Patricia Beattie Jung, and Shannon Jung, 6th ed. (Fort Worth, Texas: Harcourt Brace College Publishers, 1998), 387–405.

11. In *Ethics: A Pluralistic Approach to Moral Theory*, 2d ed. (Fort Worth, Texas: Harcourt Brace College Publishers, 1998), Lawrence M. Hinman defines ethics as "the explicit, philosophical reflection on moral beliefs and practices," while he defines morality as "the first-order beliefs and practices about good and evil by means of which we guide our behavior." He further observes, "The difference between ethics and morality is similar to the difference between musicology and music. Ethics is a conscious stepping back and reflecting on morality, just as musicology is a conscious reflection on music" (440–42). If one uses Hinman's definition, presumably a moral judgment would be a value judgment about human conduct that reflects our moral beliefs and practices, while an ethical judgment would be more contemplative in nature. This, however, draws the line somewhat more finely than is necessary in most discussions of moral issues.

12. Hinman's *Ethics* provides a useful introduction to ethical theory, including both deontological and consequentialist approaches. A particularly helpful feature of this volume is the bibliographical essay at the end of each chapter. Other useful introductions to ethical theory include William K. Frankena, *Ethics*, 2d ed. (Englewood Cliffs, N.J.: Prentice Hall, 1973); James Rachels, *The Elements of Moral Philosophy*, 2d ed. (New York: Random House, 1992); and Louis Pojman, *Ethics: Discovering Right and Wrong*, 2d ed. (Belmont, Calif.: Wadsworth, 1994).

13. Consequentialist approaches to ethics are sometimes referred to as "teleological" approaches. I find the term "consequentialist" preferable, however,

because (a) it is easier to remember, and (b) it more accurately describes this approach. The term "teleological," which comes from the Greek word for goal or objective, calls attention to the fact that this style of decision making is often directed toward accomplishing certain goals or objectives, lending moral sanction to whatever is conducive to accomplishing these goals or objectives. That is accurately descriptive in some cases. However, in other cases the side effects (what the Pentagon calls "collateral damage") are also taken into account. In such cases, the term "consequentialist" is more accurately descriptive.

14. Immanuel Kant, "On a Supposed Right to Lie from Altruistic Motives," in *Critique of Practical Reason and Other Writings in Moral Philosophy*, trans. and ed. Lewis White Beck (Chicago: University of Chicago Press, 1949), 346–50.

15. Robert Ward et al., "Infectious Hepatitis: Studies of Its Natural History and Prevention," *New England Journal of Medicine* 258, no. 9 (27 February 1958): 407–15; and Saul Krugman et al., "Infectious Hepatitis: Detection of the Virus during the Incubation Period and in Clinically Inapparent Infection," *New England Journal of Medicine* 261, no. 15 (8 October 1959): 729–34.

16. Ramsey, *Patient as Person*, 47–55.

17. Ramsey, *Patient as Person*, 55.

18. A number of examples of professional association and industry codes of ethics, as well as examples of company codes of ethics, are included in O. C. Ferrell, John Fraedrich, and Linda Ferrell, *Business Ethics: Ethical Decision Making and Cases* (Boston: Houghton Mifflin, 2002), 378–419.

19. Immanuel Kant, *Groundwork of the Metaphysics of Morals*, trans. and ed. Mary Gregor (Cambridge: Cambridge University Press, 1997), 31 (4:421). In *Groundwork of the Metaphysics of Morals*, Kant gives three different formulations of the categorical imperative. The first formulation, noted above, is restated a few sentences later as "act as if the maxim of your action were to become by your will a *universal law of nature*." The second formulation is as follows: "So act that you use humanity, whether in your own person or in the person of any other, always at the same time as an end, never merely as a means" (38 [4:429]). Kant adds a third formulation: "To do no action on any other maxim than one such that it would be consistent with it to be a universal law, and hence to act only *so that the will could regard itself as at the same time giving universal law through its maxim*" (42 [4:34]). Kant notes, "The

above three ways of representing the principle of morality are at bottom only so many formulae of the very same law, and any one of them of itself unites the other two in it" (43 [4:436]). Note: the second set of page references is to the standard German edition of Kant's works published under the auspices of the German Academy; 4:436, for example, refers to page 436 of the fourth volume of the academy edition.

20. All biblical quotations are from the New Revised Standard Version as included in *The New Oxford Annotated Bible*, ed. Bruce M. Metzger and Roland E. Murphy (New York: Oxford University Press, 1991).

21. Whether those who work in college and university dining halls and other hourly employees are entitled to receive more than the wage levels specified in their contracts has become a matter of considerable controversy at many colleges and universities.

22. The term "forbearance" is a legal term that involves the notion of exercising restraint.

23. The First Amendment to the U.S. Constitution states, "Congress shall make no law respecting an establishment of religion, or prohibiting the free exercise thereof; or abridging the freedom of speech, or of the press, or the right of the people peaceably to assemble, or to petition the government for a redress of grievances." Technically, the limitations inherent in the First Amendment guarantees pertain to what government can do, or, as the courts have ruled, to extensions of government. If you work for a private company that markets only to the general public, the protections given expression in the First Amendment to the U.S. Constitution aren't going to be of any help to you if you tell your boss to his face what you think of his new toupee.

24. A pregnant woman, however, might have contractual rights to abortion—for example, under the provisions of an insurance policy that provides coverage for abortions.

25. In *Harris v. McRae*, 448 U.S. 297 (1980), the U.S. Supreme Court upheld the Hyde amendment, which banned federal Medicaid funds for abortions not necessary to save the life of the pregnant woman. The Court ruled that even though Medicaid funds are used to pay the cost of childbirth, this doesn't extend to paying for abortions. In *Webster v. Reproductive Health Services*, 492 U.S. 490 (1989), the Court upheld a provision of a Missouri law that barred the use of public facilities for performing abortions.

26. Karl Barth, *Church Dogmatics*, vol. 2, bk. 2, trans. G. W. Bromiley et

al. (Edinburgh: T.&T. Clark, 1957), 670. Drawing upon biblical examples, Barth argues that the command of God comes concretely to each person in each situation (673). In a later volume of the same work, *Church Dogmatics,* vol. 3, bk. 4, trans. A. T. MacKay et al. (Edinburgh: T.&T. Clark, 1961), Barth moves in a more rule deontological direction as he discusses suicide, euthanasia, abortion, capital punishment, and other issues (397–470).

27. The most effective of the infiltrators were commando groups under the command of Otto Skorzeny. His operation, code-named Operation Greif (Gryphon), caused considerable consternation among American forces during the Battle of the Bulge. On one occasion, an infiltrator wearing an American uniform, when asked about the situation at the front, gave a bogus account that persuaded an American officer to withdraw his unit from the town he was defending (John S. D. Eisenhower, *The Bitter Woods* [New York: Putnam, 1969], 241). On another occasion, an infiltrator, when stopped by a sentry, surrendered and was taken to the local commander, where he confessed that he was part of the company of infiltrators commanded by Captain Stielau. To the astonishment of the prisoner, the person he had believed to be an American officer responded by saying, "So sorry, but I am a member of Stielau's company too" (Jacques Nobécourt, *Hitler's Last Gamble: The Battle of the Bulge,* trans. R. H. Barry [New York: Schocken Books, 1967], 202). The major accomplishment of the infiltrators was to unnerve American soldiers, who resorted to various word games and trivia questions to distinguish friend from foe. U.S. troops were so edgy that General Omar Bradley, who commanded U.S. forces in that sector, was stopped and interrogated by nervous sentries on three different occasions (Nobécourt, *Hitler's Last Gamble,* 200).

28. The federal regulations, which are often referred to as the Baby Doe regulations, were a response to a specific case in Bloomington, Indiana, in which a newborn infant with Down syndrome was permitted to starve to death after being denied lifesaving treatment that the parents refused to authorize. The Reagan administration initially issued regulations mandating treatment of handicapped newborn infants under the authority of section 504 of the Rehabilitation Act of 1973 (www.usdoj.gov/osg/briefs/1984/sg840041.txt [accessed 5 March 2002]). Though the U.S. Supreme Court ultimately ruled that in issuing the Baby Doe regulations the Reagan administration had overextended the authority of the Rehabilitation Act of 1973, Congress in the meantime had passed an amendment to the Child Abuse Prevention and Treatment and

Adoption Reform Act mandating treatment for most handicapped newborn infants (www.senate.gov/~rpc/rva/982/982199.htm [accessed 5 March 2002]). The major difference between the initial regulations and those mandated by Congress is that the former were implemented and monitored directly by the federal government while the latter rely on state implementation and enforcement. The federal government, however, did issue guidelines that states must follow if they are to receive federal funding for child abuse prevention programs. These guidelines mandate treatment unless "(1) the infant is chronically and irreversibly comatose; (2) the provision of such treatment would merely prolong dying or not be effective in ameliorating or correcting all of the infant's life-threatening conditions, or otherwise be futile in terms of the survival of the infant; or (3) the provision of such treatment would be virtually futile in terms of the survival of the infant and the treatment itself under such circumstances would be inhumane" (50 *Federal Register* 14878 [15 April 1985]).

29. For differing perspectives on this volatile issue, see Robert Tracinski, "The Return of the Spotted Owl: Earth First, Means Humans Last," *Capitalism Magazine,* 11 December 2000, www.capitalismmagazine.com/2000/december/rwt_spotted_owl.htm [accessed 16 August 2002]; Robert H. Nelson, "Calvinism Minus God," *Forbes,* 5 October 1998, 143; Jeanne Brokaw, "Does Anybody Give a Hoot?" *Mother Jones,* November-December 1996, 15; and Daniel Levi and Sara Kocher, "The Spotted Owl Controversy and the Sustainability of Rural Communities in the Pacific Northwest," *Environment & Behavior* 27, no. 5 (September 1995): 631–80. For a balanced analysis of the issue, see Jennifer Babson, "A Not-So-Simple Tradeoff: Regulations vs. Jobs," *Congressional Quarterly Weekly Report,* 17 June 1994, 1702–3.

30. There is an old chestnut that has been debated for years in ethics classes: how should an ethical egoist go about giving advice? Should the ethical egoist (a) advise doing what is in the best interests of the recipient of the advice, or (b) do and say whatever is most advantageous to the giver of the advice?

31. When this approach is taken, the question of whether the client actually committed the crime with which he or she has been charged is of secondary significance. Rather, the focus tends to be on attempting to persuade the judge or jury to dismiss or disregard whatever evidence the prosecuting attorney presents. In the adversarial system that is a prominent feature of both criminal and civil law, the underlying assumption is that if both sides make

the best possible case they can make, the stronger case will carry the day and justice will prevail. Whether this is actually what happens in the courtroom is open to question. There are cynics who believe that justice takes second place to lawyerly tricks and clever rhetoric that win acquittals for clients who really did the crimes of which they are accused and multimillion-dollar settlements for plaintiffs whose grievances are blown far out of proportion.

32. Though widely repeated, the slogan is not devoid of an element of ambiguity. Should the emphasis be on "the greatest good" or "the greatest number"? Suppose that a particular course of action would impose an immense cost on three individuals while resulting in limited benefit for three hundred people. Let us further suppose that when all the numbers are added up, the total benefit for the three hundred people was significantly less than the total costs imposed on the three people who would suffer as a result of what is being contemplated. Since the number of people who benefit from the action would outnumber those suffering bad results by a ratio of 100 to 1, does this mean that in keeping with the notion of "the greatest good for the greatest number," the course of action is morally justifiable? Or, in view of the fact that the total amount of good that would result would be less than the costs imposed on the unfortunate few, does this mean that the course of action is not morally justifiable?

33. Jeremy Bentham, "An Introduction to the Principles of Morals and Legislation," in *A Fragment on Government and an Introduction to the Principles of Morals and Legislation,* ed. Wilfrid Harrison (Oxford: Basil Blackwell, 1967), 125 (I, 1).

34. John Stuart Mill, "Utilitarianism," in *Utilitarianism, Liberty, and Representative Government* (London: J. M. Dent & Sons, 1910), 6.

35. See, e.g., Hinman, *Ethics,* 173–84.

36. Joseph Fletcher, *Situation Ethics: The New Morality* (Philadelphia: Westminster Press, 1966), 95.

37. Fletcher, *Situation Ethics,* 124–25.

38. In specifying the nature of the offense of "willfully disobeying" a superior commissioned officer, the Uniform Code of Military Justice states that any person is subject to this charge who "willfully disobeys a lawful command of his superior commissioned officer." (*Uniform Code of Military Justice,* sec. 890, art. 90 [2], www.military-network.com/main_ucmj/SUBCHAPTERX.html [accessed 5 March 2002]). A similar statement is made with respect to a war-

rant officer or enlisted member who willfully disobeys a warrant officer, non-commissioned officer, or petty officer.

39. See note 28 above.

40. While the notion of prima facie obligations is frequently credited to W. D. Ross, who was a rule deontologist, the usefulness of the notion is not limited to rule deontology. It is applicable to any situation in which there are competing moral considerations. For W. D. Ross's discussion of prima facie obligations, see *The Right and the Good* (Oxford: Clarendon Press, 1930), 41–47.

3

WHICH IS THE HOUSE OF TRUE MORALITY?

—

In chapter 1, reference was made to natural law theory, which holds that there is an existing moral order that is part of nature. Traditional natural law theory, as articulated by theologians and philosophers such as Augustine and Aquinas, is like a house with many rooms, each with its own character, each with many different nooks and crannies. In the rooms can be found a multitude of claims from many different eras, penned by scholars of diverse nationalities. We visited one of those rooms in chapter 1: the room containing the claim that in order for laws to be binding on conscience, they must satisfy certain moral criteria. Above the door to this room are inscribed the words of Augustine: "For a law that is unjust does not seem to me to be a law at all."

The building in which this room is to be found is the belief that there is an existing moral order in the universe, that there really are some things that are right and wrong. This moral order, referred to by many as "laws of nature" since they believe it to be part of the created natural order, comprises the floor joists and rafters that give form and strength to the building. Though the exact parameters of the building are not always seen with clarity, the foundation, walls, and roof are always there, permanent and unchanging, even as they are hit by the strong winds of change in a turbulent and tumultuous world. It is this structure that makes possible all the rooms the house contains. The words of Augustine inscribed on the plaque above the door to the room we visited might be paraphrased to read, "A room that is not inside this house is not a room at all." And indeed, it is difficult to envision a room of any sort without a structure enclosing it, thereby giving form to it.

All of this would be simple enough were there not other houses in the valley, each with its own unique structure, each incorporating and giving expression to its own set of values. Down the road a ways from the House of Natural Law is the House of Conquest, a heavily fortified gray granite building with turrets at each corner. It is an imposing structure, cold and devoid of sentiment. On the flags flapping from the turrets are the words "Might makes right." Monuments to a pantheon of military heroes dating back to ancient times line the walkway to the main entrance. Other monuments are dedicated to those who accumulated huge fortunes and used their economic power to get what they wanted. The House of Conquest is one of the oldest houses in the valley.

Immediately across the road is the House of Hedonism. The words "Eat, drink, and be merry!" are boldly proclaimed in rather garish bright red letters that stretch across the arch above the gate to the courtyard, from which raucous sounds of revelry can be heard almost any time of the day or night. It is rumored that Hugh Hefner, who founded *Playboy* magazine, had quite a bit to do with the building of several new additions to this house—and became fabulously wealthy in the process. For a number of years, Madonna and Howard Stern were frequent visitors. They still stop by from time to time, as do Ice T, the Spice Girls, the Dixie Chicks, and many other icons of contemporary culture in this era of self-gratification.

There are other houses as well, houses of many different shapes and colors. Houses with hammers and sickles and many other symbols on the flags they fly. And, making matters thoroughly confusing, there are also several houses that, like the House of Natural Law, are believed by those who inhabit them to be the House of Human Decency. They are houses built and maintained by conscientious, caring people who do not share the views of natural law theorists when it comes to a wide range of controversial issues.

Which of the many houses in the valley is the House of True Morality? Is there any way to make sense of what seems even to the most casual observer to be rampant confusion?

Natural law theorists insist that their house is the House of True Morality and that the builders and inhabitants of all the other houses are mistaken when they claim to be purveyors of true morality. And how does one discover the laws of nature that natural law theorists insist are part of an existing moral order in the universe—a moral order that, the proponents of natural law believe, makes the House of Natural Law the House of True Morality? For centuries, natural law theorists have insisted that our cognitive abilities—our abilities to think, reason, perceive, and understand—enable us to gain at least some awareness of these laws of nature. The distinguished Roman statesman and philosopher Marcus Tullius Cicero (106–43 B.C.E.), who played an important historical role in the development of natural law theory, puts it this way: "For since an intelligence common to us all makes things known to us and formulates them in our minds, honourable actions are ascribed by us to virtue, and dishonourable actions to vice; and only a madman would conclude that these judgments are matters of opinion and not fixed by nature."[1]

Aquinas speaks of "the light of natural reason, whereby we discern what is good and what is evil, which is the function of natural law." He adds that "the natural law is nothing else than the rational creature's participation of the eternal law." (Aquinas believed "that the whole community of the universe is governed by Divine Reason," which "has the nature of law" and, since it does not change, "must be called eternal.")[2] The seventeenth-century German philosopher Samuel Pufendorf (1632–94) asserts that "even if the divine revelation throws the greatest and clearest light upon the knowledge of the law of nature, it can still be investigated and definitely proved, even without such aid, by the power of reason."[3] And, to cite but one more example, the twentieth-century American theologian John Courtney Murray (1904–67), a Jesuit strongly influenced by the work of Aquinas, argues that "intelligence, with the aid of simple reasoning, can know, and know to be obligatory, a set of natural law principles."[4]

And so since antiquity, the answer that has been given by natural law theologians and philosophers to the question "How do we discover the laws of nature?" is that reason is the key to discovery. Reason provides the road map that enables us to find the House of True Morality and the key that enables us to open its door and explore the contents of its rooms.

DOES NATURE PROVIDE ANSWERS?

It is far easier, however, to claim that "the light of reason" enables us to determine that some things are good, right, and proper than it is to show how this can be done. Trying to show how this can be done is where the shoe starts pinching.

Natural law theorists, of course, have not ignored the question of how reason might enable us to determine what is good, right, and proper. Aquinas, for example, suggests that there are observable phenomena of nature that are of moral significance. He states that "inasmuch as every substance seeks the preservation of its own being, according to its nature; and by reason of this inclination, whatever is a means of preserving human life and of warding off its obstacles belongs to natural law."[5] Drawing upon a quotation attributed to sixth-century Byzantine emperor Justinian, Aquinas further suggests that "those things are said to belong to the natural law 'which nature has taught to all animals,' such as sexual intercourse, education of offspring, and so forth."[6]

On one occasion, while a class I was teaching was involved in a lively discussion about gender roles, our department secretary came to the door and informed me that I had a long-distance phone call of an urgent nature. I excused myself to take the phone call (the nature of which I no longer recall) as the students were sharply disagreeing about whether mothers have a greater obligation to take care of children than do fathers. The discussion apparently became even more heated in my absence. When I returned, a member of the class, who was somewhat of a male chauvinist, was emphatically stating, "Look at the lower animals! The female always looks after the young!"[7]

Are we to look to the field mouse for ethical guidance?

One of the practical problems inherent in attempting to derive ethical values from nature is that the laws of nature are far from clear. Disharmony is as apparent as harmony, chaos as order, and destruction as preservation. Writing more than a century ago, John Stuart Mill observed, "In sober truth, nearly all the things which men are hanged or imprisoned for doing to one another, are nature's every day performances. . . . Everything in short, which the worst men commit either against life or property is perpetrated on a larger scale by natural agents."[8]

Moreover, a number of the examples of animal behavior identifiable in nature are not likely to be accepted by many of us as models for human behavior. Male bighorn sheep delight in head-crashing duels, the echoes of their battles reverberating for miles in the clear mountain air. Lions in Africa sometimes devour their young. The pygmy hippopotamus is not noted for its industriousness. Cottontail rabbits evidence sexual behavior not likely to reduce the incidence of teenage pregnancy if practiced by humans. The female praying mantis often kills and eats her male partner after they mate, a pattern of activity that, if used as a model for human conduct, would pose quite a different set of problems. And if all of that isn't bad enough, wildlife biologist Jane Goodall tells us that chimpanzees—the species most like us in its genetic characteristics—are given to kidnapping, cannibalism, and promiscuity.[9] All things considered, it is not surprising that a study on human sexuality commissioned by the Catholic Theological Society of America a few years ago concluded that "animal behavior discloses no sexual absolutes."[10]

Those who purport to see moral values in nature tend to pick and choose. Robins and other songbirds that provide for the nutritional needs of their offspring provide a good role model. Lions that devour their young are quite a different matter. In the final analysis, those who claim to derive ethical values from nature are in reality making certain value assumptions about nature—value assumptions that provide a screen to sort out what they like from what they don't like. In short, instead of deriving ethical values from nature, they are bringing their own set of ethical values to nature and interpreting nature in light of these values.

Some might suggest that we need to go beyond the casual observations about nature made by those without scientific training and listen to what scientists have to say if we are to find answers to moral questions. An acquaintance who is strongly opposed to abortion asserts that he "knows that human life begins at conception" because he was a biology major in college and learned from his biology instructors that conception marks the beginning of human life.

But does biology really provide answers to moral questions? Those trained in the life sciences can tell us a good deal about how the genetic code is formed at conception (a process, by the way, that takes at least a day and does not occur, as many would have us believe, in a "moment"). Scientists can tell us when heart and brain activity can first be detected and when the fetus has a chance of surviving outside the womb, should birth occur. None of this, however, tells us when the life of an individual human being is first present. Nor does anything that scientists can say about the development of the fetus tell us whether ending whatever is there is morally justifiable.

Facts about fetal development assume moral significance only if one makes certain value assumptions about them. The formation of the genetic code marks the beginning of human life only if being an organism with a human genetic code is a necessary and sufficient condition for something to be a human being. If some other standard is used—for example, if it is asserted that to be a human being is to have a functioning brain—then what life scientists tell us about the formation of the genetic code, while interesting, is of no particular moral significance.

This is not to suggest that facts are irrelevant to moral inquiry. Once certain value assumptions are made, relevant facts are of tremendous significance. Suppose that one argues that if irreversible loss of brain function, including that of the brain stem, is to be the indicator of the end of human life (the legal definition of death in many states), the beginning of brain function should be viewed as the beginning of human life. Once this value claim is made, moral theologians and philosophers have a keen interest in learning from life scientists how early in the process of fetal development brain function is identifiable.

Another example of the way that science and ethics interface is provided by sustainable agriculture, a notion that has assumed increased significance in recent years as environmental concerns related to agriculture confront economic reality. Dennis R. Keeney, professor of agronomy and former director of the Leopold Center for Sustainable Agriculture at Iowa State University, defines sustainable agriculture as "agricultural systems that are environmentally sound, profitable, and productive and that maintain the social fabric of the rural community."[11] Or as poet and environmentalist Wendell Berry puts it, sustainable agriculture is "agriculture that does not deplete soils or people."[12]

Once one makes the value assumption that sustainable agriculture is an appropriate ethic for farmers, it is tremendously important to discover what the environmental impact of various pesticides is, what types and amounts of artificial fertilizers can be used without resulting in unacceptable levels of groundwater contamination, and much more. Scientists at Iowa State University and elsewhere are working on these and other matters and, by so doing, are contributing significantly to agricultural ethics.

Here as elsewhere, however, the facts about nature are of moral significance only when one makes certain value assumptions about them. Determining what types and amounts of pesticides and artificial fertilizers can be used without resulting in excessive groundwater contamination, for example, is of moral significance only if one assumes that groundwater contamination above a certain level is unacceptable.

The point to be underscored here is that when considered in isolation, science tells us nothing about what we should or should not be doing. Scientific data are of moral significance only when we make certain value assumptions about the data. Pinning down these value assumptions—and providing a rationale for accepting one set of value assumptions rather than others—is the tricky matter.

SOCIOBIOLOGY

A new twist on an old theory evoked a firestorm of controversy in 1975 when Harvard biologist Edward O. Wilson (1929–) published *Sociobiology: The New Synthesis*.[13] In this book, Wilson argues for "the morality of the gene," insisting that moral traits such as altruism can be explained by the genetic characteristics of individuals that result from the process of natural selection. He asserts that "the emotional control centers in the hypothalamus and limbic system of the brain . . . flood our consciousness with all the emotions—hate, love, guilt, fear, and others—that are consulted by ethical philosophers who wish to intuit the standards of good and evil." And what accounts for these "emotional control centers"? "They evolved by natural selection," a theme to which he returns in *On Human Nature*, a Pulitzer Prize–winning book published three years after *Sociobiology*.[14] He states in *On Human Nature*, "The genes hold culture on a leash. The leash is very long, but inevitably values will be constrained in accordance with their effects on the human gene pool. The brain is a product of evolution."[15] And with a persistence that has spanned several decades, Wilson sounds a similar theme in *Consilience: The Unity of Knowledge*. (He defines consilience as the "interlocking of causal explanation across disciplines.")[16] In this volume, he speaks of a need to fill a void in "the biology of moral sentiments" by identifying "the prescribing genes" and learning more about the development of moral sentiments resulting from the interactions of genes and the environment.[17]

I am content to leave to others the question of whether the process of natural selection indeed has resulted in genetic combinations that account for moral sentiments. Suffice it to say that even if it is the case that the values that we and others hold are determined, in whole or in part, by our genetic heritage, the question remains as to whether these values are good and right and proper. As with all other observations about nature, the fact that something exists or doesn't exist is one matter. The question of whether it is good or bad is quite another.

THE "NATURALISTIC FALLACY"

Philosophers often refer to the view that ethical values can be derived from observations of nature as a definist theory of ethics since those who take this approach assume that value terms can simply be defined in factual terms (for example, the good is that which is found in nature). Once such a definition is made, one can determine whether something is good, right, or appropriate simply by checking out the facts.

The fact that things exist or occur in a certain way, however, leaves open the question of whether they should be that way. Thus, following the lead of the British philosopher G. E. Moore (1873–1958), critics of definist theories have often decried the "naturalistic fallacy" by asserting that to attempt to define value terms in factual terms is to overlook the difference between the "is" and the "ought," between facts and values.[18] For example, we might all agree that ice cream is sweet in view of the fact that it stimulates the taste buds in a particular manner. But it still makes sense to ask, for dietary reasons as well as for reasons of personal taste, "But is it good?" If being good were simply the same as being sweet, it wouldn't make sense to ask, "This ice cream is sweet, but is it good?" since this would be the equivalent of saying, given the interchangeability of equivalent terms, "This ice cream is sweet, but is it sweet?"

Moore, it might be added, calls into question a number of popular theories about what might be discovered by studying nature. Take, for example, the widely held assumption that we can determine what constitutes good health by looking at nature. "When therefore we are told that health is natural, we may presume that what is meant is that it is normal," he observes. (By normal, he means usual and customary.) And since the diseased members of a species tend to die off while the healthy individuals survive, health, understood as the absence of disease, tends to be the statistical norm in nature. Moore, however, continues, "But is it so obvious that the normal must be good . . . ? Was the excellence of Socrates or of Shakespeare normal? Was it not rather abnormal, extraordinary?"[19]

No less devastating is his critique of the view that evolution can be equated with progress—that evolution points in the direction of that which is good. Moore states, "This is the view that we ought to move in the direction of evolution simply because it is the direction of evolution. . . . That such a view . . . is simply fallacious, I have tried to shew. It can only rest on the confused belief that somehow the good simply means the side on which Nature is working."[20] As Moore correctly notes, even if it is the case that the evolutionary processes are moving in an identifiable direction (a theory that is by no means universally held in the scientific community), it does not follow that the movement is invariably in a good direction.[21]

Wilson, it might be added, is aware that he has been criticized for running afoul of the naturalistic fallacy. In *Consilience* he responds by asserting that "the naturalistic fallacy is itself a fallacy. For if ought is not is, what is?"[22] But Wilson is too clever by half. As Moore correctly realized, just because something is the way it is doesn't mean that it is the way it ought to be.

ARE THERE "MORAL INSTINCTS"?

Intuitionism, the theory that there are certain moral truths that are known to us intuitively, is another way of trying to determine what is really right or wrong. Some hold that we all have certain built-in moral instincts that function as a "moral compass" of some sort (a view that has some similarity to Wilson's theory of genetically based moral sentiments). Aquinas, for example, suggests that "all those things to which man has a natural inclination, are naturally apprehended by reason as being good, and consequently as objects of pursuit, and their contraries as evil, and objects of avoidance."[23]

But, as with efforts to derive moral values from studies of nature, the moral instinct form of intuitionism comes with a host of question marks surrounding it. Granted, people do have tendencies to act in certain ways. Most people are inclined to view certain things as right and other things as wrong. But are these really moral instincts that can plausibly be characterized as moral intuition?

We often speak of conscience, as when we say that "my conscience won't let me do that." But when stripped to its essentials, what does conscience really involve? Are we born with certain built-in moral instincts? Or is what we identify as conscience simply a matter of social conditioning, a reflection of the way we have been brought up and the behavioral patterns we have acquired in the course of the years?

Even if it is the case that people have moral instincts that function like built-in moral compasses, we still aren't out of the woods. If all moral compasses were pointing in the same direction, we could perhaps with greater confidence speak of moral instincts and identify the path that will get us out of the woods. But unfortunately, that's not the way things work. When it comes to controversial issues such as abortion, physician-assisted suicide, and same-sex marriage, the moral compasses that various individuals believe they have point in very different directions. How do we go about determining which one is pointing in the right direction? It won't do, it might be added, to assert that those whose moral compasses point in different directions than ours are simply mistaken. Even though we might firmly believe that we are right and they are wrong, what basis do we have for saying that our moral compasses are pointing in the right direction whereas theirs are not working properly?

There is yet another matter that needs to be noted. Even if there are certain inclinations that are universal or nearly universal, that doesn't necessarily mean they are good ones. Greed, for example, is quite prevalent in many societies, including our own. But does that mean "greed is good," as convicted stock market manipulator Ivan Boesky insisted during the self-centered 1980s? Various theologians throughout the ages, including both Augustine and Aquinas, have argued that we are all sinful—that everyone is flawed. As with trying to identify appropriate moral values by observing animal behavior, determining that human beings, generally speaking, have an inclination to act in a certain manner doesn't automatically mean that this is a good inclination. It might be the reflection of a flawed human nature.

Even if we are absolutely certain that our moral compasses are pointing in the right direction, certainty of belief is not the same as knowing something intuitively. To illustrate this point, twentieth-century British philosopher W. D. Hudson poses the hypothetical example of an anguished mother whose son has been reported as having been killed in action but who firmly believes that he is still alive. If it turns out that the report was incorrect and that instead of being killed in action he is a prisoner of war, the mother, upon hearing the corrected report, would undoubtedly say, "I knew it all along." But what of the other alternative—irrefutable evidence such as the recovery of his remains that made it very clear that he indeed had died on the battlefield? Would she still say, "I knew it all along"? Probably not. Rather, Hudson suggests, she would be far more likely to say, "'I felt sure that he was alive, but now I know that he is dead.'" Hudson notes, "There are numerous examples of people feeling absolutely sure of something and being right; and apparently equally numerous examples of them so feeling and being wrong. But, as far as any evidence that is available to us may go, there does not seem to be anything necessarily different about the intuition, i.e., the feeling of certainty, in the two kinds of examples."[24]

ARE THERE SELF-EVIDENT MORAL TRUTHS?

Some assert that certain ethical claims are self-evident. Our Declaration of Independence, for example, proclaims, "We hold these truths to be self-evident, that all men are created equal, that they are endowed by their Creator with certain unalienable Rights, that among these are Life, Liberty and the pursuit of Happiness."

Simply saying that certain things are self-evident, however, doesn't automatically mean that such is the case. Granted, to those of us who firmly believe that what the Declaration of Independence says is right, the value claims made in the document might seem self-evident. But, as the eighteenth-century English theologian and philosopher Joseph Butler (1692–1752) recognized, certainty of belief is not the same as something being self-evident. Butler observes, "Indeed the truth of revealed religion, peculiarly so called, is not self-evident, but requires external proof, in order to its being received."[25]

What exactly does it mean for something to be "self-evident"? And is there any meaningful way that we can say that there are certain moral truths that are self-evident? The *Oxford English Dictionary* defines "self-evident" as "evident of itself without proof."[26] But how can something be "evident of itself without proof"?

John Locke, whose writings influenced Thomas Jefferson, the prime author of our Declaration of Independence, wrestled with this question in *An Essay Concerning Human Understanding*, published in 1690. There are some things, he allowed, that are self-evident—for example, the similarity or dissimilarity of ideas such as colors or geometrical forms. And indeed, it is quite apparent that regardless of the words that are used to give expression to the differences, a circle is not a square, a man is not a horse, and red is not blue. Locke also observed that there are certain mathematical relationships that are self-evident, such as the axiom that says that if equals are subtracted from equals, the remainders will be equal.[27]

But does saying, "It is self-evident that all human beings are created equal" have the same degree of certitude as saying, "It is self-evident that red and blue are different colors"? While many different words in many different languages are used to identify various colors, once linguistic variations are taken into account, one is hard-pressed to find anyone anywhere (at least anyone who is not color-blind) who sincerely believes that red and blue are really the same color. Locke was right. It is self-evident that red and blue are different colors.[28]

The same cannot be said, however, with respect to the claim that all human beings are created equal or any other ethical claim. Even though many of us sincerely believe that all people are born with the same basic rights, that is by no means a universally held view. One does not need to look far, either historically or in the world today, to find examples of tyrants and despots who despise the notion of equality and respect for all persons. Rejection of the notion of equal rights, it might be added, is not limited to tyrants and despots. A number of the signers of the Declaration of Independence, including Jefferson, owned slaves. The equality of all persons, it seems, was not self-evident even to them, notwithstanding the resounding endorsement of equality given expression in the ringing words of that much quoted and revered document. Like consent theories of obligation, the view that there are self-evident basic rights undoubtedly played a significant political role in the struggle to secure more democratic forms of government. But as an ethical theory, the claim that there are self-evident moral truths leaves us with a lot of unanswered questions.

DO ETHICS AND MATHEMATICS BELONG TO THE SAME CLASS?

In *Mere Christianity*, British literary critic and popular defender of Christianity C. S. Lewis (1898–1963) suggests that moral law "belongs to the same class as mathematics."[29] But is this really the case?

If ethics and mathematics really do belong in the same class, there should be plausible ways of demonstrating the validity of ethical claims that are correct, just as there are plausible ways of demonstrating the validity of mathematical claims that are correct. For example, it is possible to come up with persuasive demonstrations, such as counting on one's fingers, to demonstrate conclusively that $2 + 2 = 4$. To be sure, numbers themselves are nothing more than symbols to express quantitative relationships; many different ways of numbering things have been devised in the course of human history. The underlying quantitative relationships, however, are not simply a matter of opinion. No one would seriously argue that academic freedom would be in any way jeopardized if a teacher refused to give a passing grade to a student who insisted that $2 + 2 = 5$.

Similarly, the observation that followers of Pythagoras made in classical Greek times when they noted that the square of the hypotenuse of a right triangle is equal to the sum of the squares of the other two sides is not just something they made up. As students of geometry know, there are ways of demonstrating that this is the case. Anyone asserting that the square of the hypotenuse of a right triangle is equal to, say, twice the sum of the squares of the other two legs would not be likely to do particularly well on an exam covering that area of geometry.

But how does one demonstrate the validity of ethical claims, particularly when one gets to the level of ultimate principles? For example, how, if at all, can we prove that we ought to act in accordance with the law of love rather than act on the basis of self-interest? I know of no such proof that enables going beyond simply making a statement of belief. No educated person would insist that $2 + 2 = 5$ or deny the validity of the Pythagorean theorem about right triangles. In contrast, even the most thoughtful and highly trained philosophers and theologians disagree passionately not only about matters such as abortion, physician-assisted suicide, and same-sex marriage but also about what ought to count above all else and about what values, in the final analysis, should ultimately guide our conduct. In the case of mathematics, education results in consensus, at least when dealing with certain basic quantitative relationships. The same is not true of ethics, where differences persist and are just as noticeable—if not more noticeable—among those who are highly educated. Unless a way is discovered to demonstrate persuasively that one set of moral views is right while others are false or mistaken, putting ethics and mathematics in the same class is not warranted.

ARE THERE "ETHICAL GENIUSES"?

In a book entitled *Phenomenology of Natural Law,* Dutch philosopher William A. Luijpen (1922–) asserts that there are a few people in society with superior ethical insights. We ought to turn to the "ethical genius," he argues, to eliminate confusion about what's right and what's wrong. And how do we go about determining who is an ethical genius? Luijpen suggests that "the best members of a society themselves decide this question."[30]

But unfortunately, life isn't that simple. There are all sorts of people running around claiming to be ethical geniuses. Indeed, self-proclaimed ethical geniuses can be found on every side of every major issue facing us. As for "the best members of a society" deciding who the real ethical geniuses are, who is to say who the best members of society really are? Even if we could all agree that, say, those who pay their taxes, go to church regularly, and show up for work on time make up the best members of society, we still would not have uncovered consensus on moral issues. On many different issues, there is a wide range of opinion, even among those who pay their taxes, go to church regularly, and show up for work on time.

A "THIN THEORY OF THE GOOD"?

In *A Theory of Justice*, a book published in 1971 that was to become a benchmark for twentieth-century moral and political philosophy, Harvard philosopher John Rawls (1921–) maps out what he labels a "thin theory of the good." Its purpose, he states, is "to secure the premises about primary goods required to arrive at the principles of justice," principles that he discusses in considerable detail throughout the volume.[31] Underlying his thin theory of the good is the assumption that there are certain "primary goods" that "it is supposed a rational man wants whatever else he wants." These primary goods, he suggests, are "rights and liberties, opportunities and powers, income and wealth."[32] If a "veil of ignorance" were to prevent people from knowing what their actual social situations were, Rawls theorizes, they would opt for principles of justice such as equal liberty for all. Why? To make certain they wouldn't be shortchanged in the allocation of primary goods, in the event that once the veil of ignorance was lifted, they discovered that they were among the less privileged members of society.[33]

Though appealing in its simplicity, Rawls's thin theory of the good is flawed. His list of primary goods, which he assumes any rational person would want to have in greater measure rather than lesser measure, reflects the values of a white male living in the affluence of twentieth-century America. To characterize those values as the values that any rational person can be assumed to have flies in the face of cultural diversity. There are many individuals and groups of individuals—the Old Order Amish, for example, or those who have taken a vow of poverty upon joining a religious order—who see affluence as far less important that other considerations, be they spiritual or familial. And speaking of the latter, why does Rawls's list of primary goods not include family and friends? In short, Rawls appears to have stacked the deck to favor the principles of justice that he champions. We are left with the question of why the deck should be stacked the way he chose to stack it.

IS ETHICS SIMPLY A MATTER OF PERSONAL PREFERENCE?

Where does failure to find persuasive proof establishing the validity of one set of values, to the exclusion of all others, leave us? When all things are considered, is there nothing that is right or wrong? Is choosing the house of morality in which to live simply a matter of personal preference?

In a widely quoted passage, the twentieth-century French philosopher Jean-Paul Sartre (1905–80) asserts, "Man is nothing else but that which he makes of himself." Sartre recalls an incident in which a student came to him during the Nazi occupation of France asking for advice about a very difficult matter. The student's father was somewhat of a Nazi collaborator. His older brother had been killed during the

1940 German offensive. His grieving mother's one consolation was her remaining son, who was torn between a sense of duty to his mother and a desire to avenge the death of his older brother by going to England to join the Free French. Sartre, who himself was active in the resistance movement, makes no judgment about the father's collaboration with the Nazis. For the student seeking advice, Sartre recounts, "I had but one reply to make. You are free, therefore choose—that is to say, invent. No rule of general morality can show you what you ought to do; no signs are vouchsafed in this world."[34]

Is Sartre right? Is it simply a matter of personal preference as to whether we stay at home, fight for our country, or become a Nazi collaborator? Must we invent our own morality?

SOME ANALYTICAL DISTINCTIONS

Some analytical distinctions are helpful when responding to this question. In keeping with the basic rule of thumb that says that one should never use a simple term when a complex one will do, philosophers and theologians often make a distinction between *ontological* and *epistemological* claims. Ontological claims are claims about what exists. Epistemological claims are claims about how we go about knowing and understanding things. "Is there an existing moral order in the universe?" and "Is that which is good part of an objective reality?" are ontological questions. "Can we by using our cognitive abilities determine what is right and wrong?" and "Can we know objective claims about what is good to be true or false in a verifiable manner?" are epistemological questions. (Epistemological questions about ethics aren't quite the same as rhetorical questions about whether we can prove to the satisfaction of others that some things are right or wrong. As parents of teenagers are well aware, knowing—or at least firmly believing—that some things are right or wrong doesn't necessarily translate into being able to persuade others that these things indeed are right or wrong.)

Traditional natural law theory involves both ontological and epistemological claims. When natural law theorists claim that there is an existing moral order in the universe, they are making an ontological claim. When they suggest that by using our heads we can gain awareness of at least a portion of this existing moral order, they are making an epistemological claim.

Theologians and philosophers who address ontological issues often also make a distinction between *objectivism* and *subjectivism*. Natural law theorists, by insisting that there is an existing moral order in the universe, are objectivists because they believe that this moral order is there regardless of anything that anyone might do and regardless of whether anyone happens to be aware of it. In contrast, Sartre, by suggesting (at least in the passages noted) that "man is nothing else but that which he makes of himself" and that there are no preexisting rules of morality, is a subjectivist.[35] Subjectivism is the ethical equivalent of saying, "Beauty is in the eye of the beholder."

Yet another analytical distinction is useful. Philosophers and theologians who address epistemological issues of relevance for ethics often make a distinction between *value cognitivist* and *value noncognitivist* theories. Value cognitivists such as the traditional natural law theorists hold that by using our heads, we can come to know at least some things that are good, right, and proper. In contrast, value noncognitivists suggest that our cognitive abilities do not enable us conclusively to determine that some ethical views are right while others are false or mistaken. For the value noncognitivist, "knowing" is more closely akin to "believing" than to "having uncovered" or "having discovered."

If one is to be a value cognitivist on the epistemological level, one also has to be an objectivist on the ontological level. Why? Because it makes sense to claim that by using our heads we can gain awareness of an existing moral order only if there is an existing moral order of which to gain awareness. It does not follow, however, that if one is a value noncognitivist on the epistemological level, one has to be a subjectivist on the ontological level. The fact that we cannot prove that certain things are right or wrong does not by implication suggest that the only ethical values that exist are the ones we create for ourselves. The failure of natural law theorists to demonstrate persuasively that ethical values can be derived from nature or that there are self-evident moral truths does not by implication mean that ethics is just a matter of personal opinion. Nor does it mean that when push comes to shove, it doesn't make any difference what we do.

The bottom line in all of this is that we have to be just as careful about what we deny as about what we claim. For example, the fact that we can't prove that there is life in other solar systems does not prove that no such life exists. Similarly, the fact that we can't prove that love and respect for our fellow human beings, rather than greed, selfishness, and indifference, ought to be the primary ethical values guiding our conduct doesn't mean that it's all six of one and half a dozen of the other. The fact that reason alone cannot conclusively determine which house in the valley is the House of True Morality does not by implication mean that no House of True Morality exists and that it doesn't make any difference which house we inhabit.

This is not to suggest that reason has no role to play in ethics. The rules of logic stand in the way of our taking positions inconsistent with the ethical values we affirm. For example, to claim that we care about our fellow human beings and then do things harmful to others flies in the face of logic by violating the principle of consistency. But when we get to the question of what counts above all else—the question of ultimate values—reason can no longer help us. At this point, either we must opt for subjectivism, saying that the only values that exist are those we create for ourselves and that there really isn't anything that is right or wrong, or we must enter the realm of faith. I am inclined toward the latter.

CENTERS OF VALUE

Sometimes the faiths we espouse are religious in nature. Sometimes they are completely secular. Sometimes the faith that is affirmed is part of a belief system shared by a community. Sometimes it is simply a matter of personal belief. But regardless of whether a particular person's faith is religious or secular, part of a shared set of beliefs or individualistic in nature, it involves affirming and accepting as true things she or he cannot absolutely prove to be true. And it involves allowing these beliefs to give shape, substance, and direction to one's life. Such being the case, a confession of faith must always be made in the first person singular, even if others share the beliefs, for believing is something each person must do for himself or herself.

In an insightful essay entitled "Faith in Gods and in God," H. Richard Niebuhr (1894–1962) uses the language of "the center of value" to explain what faith involves. He speaks of "the faith that life is worth living, or better, the reliance on certain centers of value as able to bestow significance and worth on our existence."[36] Many, he suggests elsewhere in his writings, are polytheists in the sense that they attempt to have multiple centers of value, "referring now to this and now to that valued being as the source of life's meaning. Sometimes they live for Jesus' God, sometimes for country and sometimes for Yale."[37] (Niebuhr taught at Yale University—hence the reference to Yale.)

Niebuhr suggests that everyone has a center of value of some sort. "For no man," he states, "lives without living for some purpose, for the glorification of some god, for the advancement of some cause."[38] In this he may have been mistaken. There are those who appear to have no discernible core of values that give form to their lives (unless, perhaps, being valueless itself is a value). At least to the outside observer, they seem to embrace no meaning or purpose to life whatsoever.[39]

Niebuhr nevertheless was correct in characterizing faith as the experience of living one's life informed and guided by some sort of a center of value that gives direction to one's life and establishes priorities by indicating what counts above all else. And he was also correct in reminding us that faith, properly understood, isn't limited to adhering to the beliefs and practices of an organized religion or to being a theist, though there certainly are members of organized religions and other theists who are people of faith.

As for my own confession of faith, I firmly believe that people count and that all of our fellow human beings are worthy of our respect, regardless of who they are and what views they espouse, for each person is precious in God's eyes. I firmly believe that, in keeping with the Ten Commandments, we ought not ride roughshod over our fellow human beings and that the claims about rights given expression in our Declaration of Independence and Bill of Rights are of profound ethical significance. I firmly believe that compassion and respect for our fellow human beings, rather than harshness and indifference, ought to typify our conduct and that simply to live for self-serving economic gain, motivated by greed and selfishness, is to live a very hollow existence. I firmly believe that the prophet Micah got it right more than twenty-five centuries ago when he asked rhetorically, "And what does the Lord require of you but to do justice, and to love kindness, and to walk humbly with your God?" (Micah 6.8).

When giving expression to our individual confessions of faith, we can often describe them in great detail and note the implications that they have for the way that we live our lives. We can tell of our childhood years and family influences, of the communities that have nurtured us and the events that have shaped our lives. We can recount the crises we have endured and the soul-searching we have experienced. In short, we can give a full or partial account of the things that have made us, to use theologian James M. Gustafson's phrase, "the sort of person" that we are.[40] But that is all we can do. Once we have given full expression to our individual confessions of faith and explained as best we can how it is that we came to hold these particular articles of faith, we can do no more than say with the Protestant reformer Martin Luther (1483–1546), "Here I stand."[41]

Ten Questions for Reflection and Discussion

1   In a pluralistic society in which there are many different views about what is ethical, how should we go about determining what is right and what is wrong?

2   Is there really anything that is right or wrong? Or is what is right or wrong nothing more than personal opinion?

3   If there is an existing moral order in the universe, is there any way that we can determine its content?

4   What, if anything, can we learn about ethics by studying nature?

5   Is there such a thing as moral intuition? If so, how does it work?

6   Are people born with a conscience? If so, what is the nature of conscience? And why do the needles of the moral compasses of various individuals point in different directions?

7   Are ethical values genetically determined?

8   Are there self-evident moral truths? If so, what are some examples? And is it possible to demonstrate that they are self-evident?

9   Do ethics and mathematics belong in the same class?

10   Do those who are better educated have better ethical values than those with less education?

NOTES

1. Cicero, *De Legibus,* trans. Clinton Walker Keyes, Loeb Classical Library (Cambridge: Harvard University Press, 1928), 347 (I, xvi, 44–45).

2. Thomas Aquinas, *Summa Theologica,* trans. Fathers of the English Dominican Province (New York: Benziger, 1947), I-II, Q.91, A.2.

3. Samuel Pufendorf, *De Jure Naturae et Gentium Libri Octo,* vol. 2, trans. C. H. Oldfather and W. A. Oldfather (Oxford: Clarendon Press, 1934), 201 (D, 3, 13).

4. John Courtney Murray, S.J., "Natural Law and Public Consensus," in *Natural Law and Modern Society,* ed. John Cogley (Cleveland: World, 1966), 63.

5. Aquinas, *Summa Theologica,* I-II, Q.94, A.2.

6. Aquinas, *Summa Theologica,* I-II, Q.94, A.2.

7. This anecdote and some of the themes developed in this chapter are noted in one of my previous books, *Hope Is Where We Least Expect to Find It* (Lanham, Md.: University Press of America, 1993), 12–17.

8. John Stuart Mill, "Nature," in *Three Essays on Religion: Nature, the Utility of Religion, and Theism* (London: Longmans, Green, 1923), 28–30.

9. Jane Goodall, "Life and Death at Gombe," *National Geographic,* May 1979, 593–621.

10. Anthony Kosnik et al., *Human Sexuality: New Directions in American Catholic Thought* (New York: Paulist Press, 1977), 64.

11. Dennis R. Keeney, "Toward a Sustainable Agriculture: Need for Clarification of Concepts and Terminology," *American Journal of Alternative Agriculture* 4, nos. 3–4 (1989): 102.

12. Quoted in Keeney, "Toward a Sustainable Agriculture," 102.

13. Edward O. Wilson, *Sociobiology: The New Synthesis* (Cambridge: Harvard University Press, Belknap Press, 1975). For an overview of the controversy surrounding this book, including a sharply worded letter to the editor printed in *New York Review of Books* and Wilson's response to it, see Arthur L. Caplan, ed., *The Sociobiology Debate: Readings on Ethical and Scientific Issues* (New York: Harper & Row, 1978).

14. Wilson, *Sociobiology,* 3.

15. Edward O. Wilson, *On Human Nature* (Cambridge: Harvard University Press, 1978), 167.

16. Edward O. Wilson, *Consilience: The Unity of Knowledge* (New York: Vintage Books, 1998), 8–14, 359.

17. Wilson, *Consilience,* 279.

18. Moore's critique of naturalism is to be found in *Principia Ethica* (Cambridge: Cambridge University Press, 1960), see esp. 9–17 and 37–58. William K. Frankena provides a very readable discussion of the open-question argument in *Ethics,* 2d ed. (Englewood Cliffs, N.J.: Prentice-Hall, 1963), 80–83. See also R. M. Hare's discussion of definist theories in *The Language of Morals* (New York: Oxford University Press, 1964), 79–93.

19. Moore, *Principia Ethica,* 42–43.

20. Moore, *Principia Ethica,* 56. Moore, it might be added, is sometimes characterized as an intuitionist who believed that we can intuitively determine what is right and what is wrong. It is debatable as to whether that is an accurate reading of Moore. In the preface to *Principia Ethica,* Moore notes that while he sometimes uses the language of intuitionism, "I beg it may be noticed that I am not an 'Intuitionist,' in the ordinary sense of the term." As for propositions asserting that a certain action is a right or duty, he emphasizes, "Again, I would wish it observed that, when I call such propositions 'Intuitions,' I mean *merely* to assert that they are incapable of proof; I imply nothing whatever as to the manner or origin of our cognition of them" (x).

21. See, e.g., Stephen Jay Gould, *Full House: The Spread of Excellence from Plato to Darwin* (New York: Harmony Books, 1996), 19–20, 169–75. Gould asserts, "Humans are here by the luck of the draw, not the inevitability of life's direction or evolution's mechanism" (175).

22. Wilson, *Consilience,* 273.

23. Aquinas, *Summa Theologica,* I-II, Q.94, A.2.

24. W. D. Hudson, *Modern Moral Philosophy* (Garden City, N.Y.: Doubleday, 1970), 101–4.

25. Joseph Butler, *The Analogy of Religion Natural and Revealed to the Constitution and Course of Nature* (London: George Routledge & Sons, 1887), 275–76 (II, conc.).

26. *Oxford English Dictionary,* 2d ed., s.v. "self-evident."

27. John Locke, *An Essay Concerning Human Understanding,* ed. Peter H. Nidditch (Oxford: Clarendon Press, 1975), 591–94 (iv, vii, 1–7). The prevailing epistemological theme in Locke's *Essay Concerning Human Understanding* is the assertion that knowledge is gained via experience. He argues,

"Let us then suppose the Mind to be, as we say, white Paper, void of all Characters, without any *Ideas,* How comes it to be furnished . . .? To this I answer, in one word. From *Experience:* In that, all our Knowledge is founded; and from that it ultimately derives its self" (104; ii, i, 2). In discussing self-evident truths, Locke, in effect, is contending that even if there are self-evident truths (which he is willing to concede), that does not stand in the way of saying that all knowledge comes from experience. In response to those who contended that (a) maxims and other self-evident truths are known to the mind prior to and quite apart from experience and (b) other parts of knowledge can be derived from these maxims, Locke insists, *"First,* That they are not the *Truths first known* to the Mind, is evident to Experience. . . . *Secondly,* From what has been said, it plainly follows, that these magnified *Maxims,* are not the Principles and *Foundations* of all our other *Knowledge"* (595–96; iv, vii, 9–10).

28. Things that are self-evident are not always immediately apparent. A while back as I was reading an article on the Pythagoreans of ancient Greece, I happened upon an observation they had made about the relationship between the length of a string of a stringed instrument and the pitch of the sound that it makes. They observed that if the length of the string is reduced to half its length, the pitch of the sound it makes will be one octave higher. Though I have played a guitar since childhood, that relationship had escaped my notice. When I went home that evening, I grabbed a tape measure and pulled out my guitar. The Pythagoreans were right. The fret that produces a pitch one octave higher than the pitch sounded by an open string is exactly at the midpoint between the nut on the neck of the guitar over which the strings run and the bridge of the guitar.

29. C. S. Lewis, *Mere Christianity* (New York: Macmillan, 1952), 24–25. He gives two reasons for this conclusion. One is that "though there are differences between the moral ideas of one time or country and those of another, the differences are not really very great—not nearly so great as most people imagine—and you can recognize the same law running through all of them." The other reason, he suggests, relates to the notion of moral progress. "Progress means not just changing," he argues, "but changing for the better. If no set of moral ideas were truer or better than any other, there would be no sense in preferring civilised morality to savage morality, or Christian morality to Nazi morality."

30. William A. Luijpen, *Phenomenology of Natural Law,* trans. Henry J. Koren (Pittsburgh: Duquesne University Press, 1967), 179, 196.

31. John Rawls, *A Theory of Justice* (Cambridge: Harvard University Press, Belknap Press, 1971), 396. In their final formulation, Rawls's two principles of justice are stated as follows:

> *First Principle*
> Each person is to have an equal right to the most extensive total system of equal basic liberties compatible with a similar system of liberty for all.
>
> *Second Principle*
> Social and economic inequalities are to be arranged so that they are both to the greatest benefit of the least advantaged, consistent with the just savings principle, and attached to offices and positions open to all under conditions of fair equality of opportunity. (302)

32. Rawls, *Theory of Justice,* 92.

33. Rawls, *Theory of Justice,* 136–42.

34. Jean-Paul Sartre, "Existentialism Is a Humanism," trans. Philip Mairet, in *Existentialism from Dostoevsky to Sartre,* ed. Walter Kaufmann (Cleveland: World, 1956), 290–91.

35. While Sartre's "Existentialism Is a Humanism" is widely quoted, some philosophers believe that it is, in some ways, an inaccurate representation of some of the central themes of existentialism. In the introduction to *Existentialism from Dostoevsky to Sartre,* Kaufmann, while acknowledging the popularity of the essay, states, "This is rather unfortunate because it is after all only an occasional lecture which, though brilliant and vivid in places and unquestionably worthy of attention, bears the stamp of the moment. It contains unnecessary misstatements of fact as well as careless and untenable arguments and a definition of existentialism which has been repudiated by Jaspers and Heidegger, and ought to be repudiated by Sartre, too, because it is no less unfair to his own thought" (45). While this is not the place to get into a debate about the correct interpretation of Sartre's version of existentialism, it should be noted that passages that point in the direction of subjectivism are not limited to "Existentialism Is a Humanism." See, e.g., Sartre's *Being and Nothingness: An*

Essay on Phenomenological Ontology, trans. Hazel E. Barnes (New York: Washington Square Press, 1966), 113–14.

36. H. Richard Niebuhr, "Faith in Gods and in God," in *Radical Monotheism and Western Culture* (New York: Harper & Brothers, 1960), 117–18.

37. H. Richard Niebuhr, *The Meaning of Revelation* (New York: Macmillan, 1962), 77. In addition to monotheism and polytheism, Niebuhr speaks of "henotheism," which he defines as being "loyal to one god among many" *(Radical Monotheism and Western Culture,* 24).

38. Niebuhr, "Faith in Gods and in God," 118.

39. In a study dating back to the 1960s reported in *The Uncommitted: Alienated Youth in American Society* (New York: Harcourt, Brace, & World, 1965), psychologist Kenneth Keniston suggests that a good many people live for no discernible purpose whatsoever, an approach to life he labels "native existentialism." He comments, "Philosophically the core of this native existentialism is the denial of the inherent meaning to man's life or the universe: in a universe without structure, regularity or purpose, the center of whatever meaning can exist must inevitably be the solitary individual, isolated, gloomy, apprehensive, wary of appearances, and heeding primarily the needs of the moment" (64).

40. James M. Gustafson, *Can Ethics Be Christian?* (Chicago: University of Chicago Press, 1975), 25.

41. Luther is widely believed to have made this statement when, standing before Emperor Charles V at the Diet at Worms in 1521, he was asked to recant statements and writings critical of doctrines and practices of the Roman Catholic Church. He refused to do so, concluding his statement of refusal by saying, "My conscience is captive to the Word of God. Thus I cannot and will not recant, for going against my conscience is neither safe nor salutary. I can do no other, here I stand, God help me. Amen." (Quoted by Heiko A. Oberman in *Luther: Man between God and the Devil,* trans. Eileen Walliser-Schwarzbart [New Haven: Yale University Press, 1989], 203). Whether Luther actually made the "here I stand" statement at the Diet of Worms, however, is open to question. The phrase first appears in a version of his remarks printed in Wittenberg several years after the Diet at Worms. See, e.g., Oberman, *Luther,* 343 n. 2; and Martin Brecht, *Martin Luther: His Road to Reformation: 1483–1521,* trans. James L. Schaaf (Philadelphia: Fortress Press, 1985), 537 n. 24.

4

BUT ISN'T FAITH DANGEROUS?

—

And so the quest for answers to questions of obligation is thrust into the realm of faith, which is where a lot of folks start getting a bit uncomfortable—sometimes more than a bit uncomfortable. There are reasons for that. Repeatedly in the course of the centuries that have shaped modernity, those who fancied that they could see the world through the eyes of faith have set themselves up on pedestals. From their self-appointed places on pedestals that are nothing more than figments of their imaginations, they have proceeded to condemn everyone in sight, sometimes brutally destroying those who have a different vision of what ought to count above all else. Is faith dangerous? It can be if not properly understood. As will be suggested later in this chapter, faith is best understood within the context of humility. That, however, is not the way faith has always been understood. Historical examples such as the Spanish Inquisition illustrate the way that what begins as faith sometimes becomes arrogance—very dangerous arrogance. It is instructive to look at a couple of historical examples.

THE SPANISH INQUISITION

Though Christopher Columbus made no mention of it in his journal, the roads in southern Spain were crowded as he traveled from Granada to Palos to prepare the *Niña,* the *Pinta,* and the *Santa Maria* for what turned out to be one of the most epic voyages of all time. There was a reason the roads were crowded. On March 31, 1492, Ferdinand and Isabella, the fervently devout Roman Catholic rulers of Aragon and Castile who desired to see those they ruled united in the faith of the One Holy Catholic and Apostolic Church, had signed a decree that disrupted the lives of many of their subjects. The decree gave all Jews living in their territories four months to accept Christian baptism or leave the country—a land where for centuries Spanish Jews and their forebears had contributed greatly to the economic and cultural landscape.[1] The document was inscribed, according to one historian, with the same pen that was used to draw up the surrender document for Granada, the last Moorish stronghold on the Iberian Peninsula, and the agreement with Columbus authorizing his expedition to find a westward passage to the Indies.[2]

Though Catholic clerics proclaimed the virtues of Christianity in synagogues, on street corners, and wherever else they thought they could find an audience, most of the Spanish descendants of Abraham, Isaac, and Jacob chose to remain true to the faith of their parents and grandparents. And so, as Columbus made his way to Palos, the roads leading to the coastal cities of southern Spain were crowded with thousands of refugees, some young, some old, some on foot, some riding donkeys or whatever other beasts of burden were available to give rest to their weary feet.[3] Columbus's tiny flotilla raised sail and cast off from their moorings a half hour before sunrise on August 3, 1492—the day after the deadline the Spanish sovereigns had given their Jewish subjects to convert to Christianity or leave the country of their birth.[4]

The Jews leaving Spain, who numbered more than 160,000, made their way by whatever means they could to northern Africa, to Turkey, or wherever else they could find haven. Many died of hunger and disease. Those fortunate enough to survive were often victimized by thieves and other barbarians who took cruel advantage of them. Some, in desperation, converted to Christianity in the hope that they would be allowed to return to the homes they had left.[5]

For the *conversos*—the Jews who had converted to Christianity and, as a result, had been allowed to remain in Spain—the situation was not all that much better. For many, it was much worse, for by converting to Christianity they came under the jurisdiction of the Inquisition.

The early church, which did not have access to the coercive power of government prior to the time Christianity became the official religion of the Roman Empire, relied on persuasion to root out what was perceived as erroneous belief. But in time, harsher measures were espoused. A letter attributed to Pope Liberius (352–66) listed confiscation of property, beating, and condemnation to perpetual exile as appropriate disciplinary measures for those guilty of heresy. A twelfth-century church council in Reims prescribed branding with a hot iron and imprisonment for heretics.[6] By the middle of the thirteenth century, inquisitors, with a variety of tools at their disposal, including burning at the stake, were at work in many parts of Europe.

When the Spanish Inquisition tore apart the social fabric of Spain in the fifteenth and sixteenth centuries, conversos were not the only victims. As the Protestant movement gained momentum in the sixteenth century, those suspected of being *Luteranismo* caught the eye of inquisitors.[7] The fury of the Inquisition was visited on Juan de Vergara, one of Spain's leading intellectuals; Luis de León, a professor at the University of Salamanca; and Bartolemé Carranza, archbishop of Toledo, among others.[8] But while conversos, who were suspected of privately continuing Jewish practices behind a veneer of Christianity, were by no means the only victims of the Spanish Inquisition, they were singled out for special attention in a country in which anti-Semitism ran rampant.

Heading up the Spanish Inquisition during its period of greatest activity was Tomás de Torquemada, who, as grand inquisitor, wielded tremendous power. Born in 1420 in the Castilian town of Valladolid, Torquemada, like Thomas Aquinas two centuries before him, came from a family of nobility. And like Aquinas, he entered the Dominican order at an early age. Torquemada's decision to join the Dominican order was apparently influenced by his uncle, Juan de Torquemada, an eminent Dominican theologian who served as cardinal of San Sisto. The younger Torquemada gained a reputation for proficiency in theology. Though he preferred to devote his time to theology, he was named prior of the convent of Santa Cruz at Segovia, a position he accepted with reluctance and held for twenty-two years.

One doesn't have to look far in the history of Christianity (or any other major religion) to find shallow, ambitious individuals who have used ecclesiastical structures for self-serving purposes as they have grasped for power and prominence. Torquemada, however, wasn't that sort of person. Rather, he was a person of deep conviction and austere ways (he never ate meat, wore linen clothing, or used linen on his bed) with single-minded devotion to the church he cherished.[9] And indeed it was precisely this love for his church that provided the motivation for his role in the Spanish Inquisition. He was convinced that the health and wholeness of the church he loved so much could be preserved only by removing from its body the malignant tumors of heresy that, he was persuaded, afflicted it and threatened its survival.

Torquemada served as the confessor of Isabella of Castile for several years before she ascended to the throne of Castile. When Isabella and her husband, Ferdinand of Aragon, became the sovereigns of Spain, Torquemada's influence grew as he became an influential counselor in the royal court. In 1474, Ferdinand and Isabella requested, via an intermediary, that Pope Sixtus IV authorize a tribunal of Inquisition in Castile to get rid of heresy *"por via del fuego"*—"by the way of fire." Their request was granted.[10] Upon recommendation of the Spanish sovereigns, the pope in 1483 designated Torquemada the grand inquisitor for Castile and, shortly thereafter, for Aragon as well. In this capacity, Torquemada reorganized the Inquisition by setting up tribunals in several different cities and by issuing instructions for the inquisitors in the territories under his jurisdiction, specifying what aberrations of belief should be of concern to the tribunals and how the tribunals should go about conducting their inquiries.[11]

Today, many believe that the Spanish Inquisition was a kangaroo court that snatched suspected heretics from their homes without warning and, with no semblance of due process, burned them at the stake. Such was not the case. The procedure would begin with a sermon on heresy and a declaration of an Edict of Grace to allow time—usually somewhere between two weeks and several months—for voluntary confession (as well as the identification of those suspected of heresy).[12] All evidence collected via confessions or denunciations was carefully recorded and evaluated. If theological consultants agreed that the evidence seemed to suggest heresy, the inquisitorial prosecutor issued an order to arrest the suspect, who, upon being arrested, was imprisoned until the hearings were completed—a process that could take several years. After being arrested, the accused would be offered an opportunity to confess and repent. In contrast to what is widely assumed to be the case, the primary purpose of the Spanish Inquisition was penitential rather than judicial.[13]

The inquisitors could use torture, though this means of securing a confession was infrequently used (far less frequently than by secular courts of that time). If the accused did not confess, he or she would then be informed of the formal charges being made. The accused, who was permitted legal counsel, was presented with the evidence collected (with the identify of witnesses omitted) and given an opportunity to respond.[14]

No one knows for sure how many were brought before tribunals of the Spanish Inquisition. Most estimates are in the tens of thousands.

Many were acquitted of the charges brought against them. Some who confessed were judged to be sufficiently penitent, requiring no further action. Some who were found guilty of heresy were subjected to lesser penalties such as being required to wear a distinctive garment (the *sanbenito*) on various liturgical occasions to call public attention to their guilt. And some were burned at the stake. During Torquemada's fifteen-year tenure as grand inquisitor, somewhere between two thousand and three thousand unfortunate souls suffered this terrible fate.[15]

THE SERVETUS AFFAIR

Roman Catholics today are quick to remind us that the Inquisition ended years ago and that those accused of heresy are no longer burned at the stake. They are, of course, absolutely right about that.[16] Roman Catholics sometimes also point out that during the days of the Inquisition the Catholic Church was not the only branch of Christendom that put people to death. As the case of Michael Servetus (1511–53) illustrates, they are right about that as well.

Servetus, as the eminent church historian Roland Bainton (1894–1984) put it, had "the singular distinction of having been burned by the Catholics in effigy and by the Protestants in actuality."[17] Born in Aragon early in the sixteenth century, Servetus in 1531 published *Seven Books on the Errors of the Trinity*, a work in which he took issue with the traditional Christian doctrine of the Trinity. Catholic and Protestant theologians alike lost no time attacking him. Servetus responded with *Two Dialogues on the Trinity* in 1532, in which he argued that the doctrinal development of the church had strayed from the teachings of Jesus.[18]

As controversy surrounding his writings became even more heated, he decided, with somewhat uncharacteristic prudence, that wisdom was on the side of getting out of the public eye, at least for a while. He assumed the pseudonym Michel de Villeneuve and went to Paris, where he studied medicine and discovered the pulmonary circulation of blood three-quarters of a century before William Harvey.[19]

But though enjoying success in the field of medicine, he couldn't keep his mind—or his hands—off theology and, in 1553, published *The Restoration of Christianity.* While the work was still in manuscript form, he sent a copy to John Calvin (1509–64), the stern, Geneva-based reformer who was to have a huge impact on the development of several different branches of Protestantism. Why Servetus did this is unclear. How Calvin responded is very clear. Perhaps hoping to rescue Servetus from what Calvin believed was heresy, he sent Servetus a copy of the latest edition of *Institutes of the Christian Religion,* a work that defined in detail Calvin's own views. Servetus, never known for tact, returned the copy to Calvin with insulting comments written in the margins.[20] Despite Servetus's repeated requests that this material be returned to him, Calvin kept it and declared to an associate that if Servetus should ever come to Geneva, "I will not suffer him to get out alive."[21]

Calvin forwarded his correspondence with Servetus to a friend in France, who passed it on to the Inquisition tribunal in Lyon.[22] The result was that Servetus was arrested and convicted of heresy, largely on the basis of the evidence Calvin supplied. The tribunal condemned Servetus to death "by slow fire." By the time the verdict and sentence were announced, however, Servetus had escaped from prison by tricking a jailer into giving him the keys to the prison. With Servetus no longer in their custody, the tribunal had to settle for burning a picture of him, along with five bales of blank paper, the latter being burned for reasons that remain obscure.[23]

Curiosity seems to have gotten the better of Servetus after his escape from prison. Instead of going to a safe haven, as common sense would have suggested, he went to Calvin's Geneva, where, the day after he arrived, he was spotted attending a worship service Calvin was conducting. At Calvin's instigation, Servetus was arrested and again put on trial for his unorthodox views. Shortly after his arrest, Calvin stated in a letter to an associate, "I hope the judgment will be capital."[24]

At the lengthy trial, Servetus was given substantial opportunity to state his views. (At one point when he asserted that children could not commit mortal sins, Calvin reportedly responded, "He is worthy that the little chickens, all sweet and innocent as he makes them, should dig out his eyes a hundred thousand times.")[25] Servetus argued his case to no avail, however. The tribunal sentenced him to be burned at the stake. His crime, in the judgment of the tribunal, was "blasphemies against the Holy Trinity, against the Son of God, against the baptism of infants and the foundations of the Christian religion."[26]

Calvin did make an effort to have Servetus beheaded, rather than burned at the stake, but that request was not granted.[27] On October 27, 1553, Servetus was led to a pile of green wood, where he was tied to a stake with an iron chain. A stout rope was wound around his neck several times. His executioner placed on his head a crown of straw and leaves sprinkled with sulfur. When the executioner brought the torch to light the fire, Servetus let out a horrible shriek. As the fire burned, he cried, "O Jesus, Son of the Eternal God, have pity on me!" Half an hour after the fire was lit, he was dead.[28]

William Farel, one of Calvin's associates who was present at Servetus's execution, observed that Servetus might have been saved if he had described Christ as the "Eternal Son" rather than as the "Son of the Eternal God."[29] Of such semantic distinctions inquisitions are sometimes made and blood is sometimes shed.

ARROGANCE AND HUMILITY

Today, we recoil with horror when we read of the Spanish Inquisition and of the brutal execution of Servetus. And because what happened was so distressing, we try to put as much distance as possible between ourselves and those terrible events. One way that we attempt to accomplish this psychologically is to view Torquemada, Calvin, and the others responsible for similar atrocities as utterly wicked, depraved individuals totally devoid of any semblance of humanity—and most assuredly far different from the sort of people we are today.[30]

While stripping perpetrators of atrocities of their humanity might make it easier for us to deal psychologically with what happened, the truth of the matter is that neither Torquemada nor Calvin was a wild-eyed, deranged fanatic totally devoid of human sensitivity and sensibility. As already noted, the Spanish Inquisition under Torquemada's jurisdiction was directed more toward securing the repentance of those holding divergent views than toward their destruction. And as those familiar with Calvin's writings know, there are many passages encouraging compassion. For example, Calvin admonished his fellow Christians to "love those who hate us." He added, "It is that we remember not to consider men's evil intention but to look upon the image of God in them, which cancels and effaces their transgressions, and with its beauty and dignity allures us to love and embrace them."[31]

Cynics might argue that passages such as this one suggest that Calvin was a terrible hypocrite, since he didn't exactly embrace Servetus in the arms of love. While there is a case to be made for charging Calvin with hypocrisy, to simply attack Calvin as a hypocrite is to miss the point. A key element in the explosive crucible that resulted in the execution of Servetus was a belief that he posed a threat to the well-being of Christendom. As one historian said of Calvin, "To him it was all so perfectly clear that the majesty of God, the salvation of souls, and the stability of Christendom were at stake."[32] The same could be said of Torquemada, who sincerely believed that by doing everything he could to stamp out what he perceived to be heresy, he was serving the church to which he was so devoted, thereby doing that which was good and right and proper.

I should add that it is not clear to me whether Torquemada and Calvin were in fact absolutely certain about the theological claims they made or whether their assertions of certitude were smoke screens to cover up their doubts. Sometimes those who are very outspoken harbor inner doubts that torment them. Presenting a façade of certainty can be a way of trying to deal with these fears and doubts. I sing in a couple of choral groups and am struck by the fact that sometimes those who sing the loudest are those who don't know the music. They somehow seem to think that if they turn up the volume a few notches, they can persuade themselves that they really do know the music—the musical equivalent of whistling in the dark to try to allay fears and apprehensions. It has also been my observation that the most open-minded and down-to-earth people in academia, the business world, and elsewhere are often those with high levels of self-confidence—confidence in their abilities and a clear sense that they are headed in the right direction. In contrast, sometimes those who are the most threatened by—and hence intolerant of—the views of others are those with high levels of insecurity. They are the ones most likely to play authority games of various types as they try to reassure themselves by throwing their weight around.

Could the harsh actions taken by Torquemada and Calvin have been born, not of certainty of belief, but of doubt and insecurity? At this point in time, there quite obviously is no way that we can get inside their heads and come up with answers to this question. But I can't help wondering about these matters.

Though the examples that have been cited in this chapter have come from the history of Christianity, presumptions of certainty of belief destructive of other people, whether real or façades covering up insecurity, are not unique to Christianity. Ayatollah Ruhollah Khomeini (1900–1989), a Shiite Moslem who ruled Iran with an iron hand from 1979 until his death in 1989, and various leaders of many other religious traditions, have, with presumptions of certitude similar to those of Torquemada and Calvin, taken harsh measures to stifle voices of dissent. (It should also be noted that whether one is looking at Islam, Judaism, Christianity, or any other major religion, there are also gentle voices of compassion to be found—for example, St. Francis of Assisi [1182–1226].)

Both Torquemada and Calvin had what they seemed to think was a "God's-eye" view of the truth. As the twentieth-century French philosopher Maurice Merleau-Ponty (1908–61) reminds us, operating on the assumption that we have all the answers is inherently dangerous. He observes that "if I believe that I can rejoin the absolute principle of all thought . . . the suffering I create turns into happiness, ruse becomes reason, and I piously cause my adversaries to perish."[33] What Torquemada and Calvin thought was faith was, in reality, arrogance—very dangerous arrogance.

Reinhold Niebuhr (1892–1971), one of the most significant twentieth-century American theologians, warned repeatedly of the dangers of the sin of pride. He spoke of several different forms of this sin, among them pride of power (overestimating how powerful we are), pride of knowledge (overestimating how much we know) and pride of virtue (overestimating how good we are).[34] With the hindsight of history, it is easy to see in Torquemada and Calvin the sins of pride of virtue and pride of knowledge (and probably the sin of pride of power as well).

To retroactively apply Niebuhr's views about human nature to figures from the past, however, is to overlook the main point of his analysis. Niebuhr's concern was the present and the future—in short, those of us living in the here and now rather than distant figures from the past. And, he insisted, the various forms of the sin of pride are flaws present, to varying degrees, in all of us.

If Niebuhr's analysis of human nature is right—and I believe that it is—there is a little of Torquemada and Calvin in each of us, even though we would all like to think otherwise. This is not to suggest, of course, that we are in any way supportive of atrocities such as burning at the stake those whose views differ from ours. Thank goodness that freedom of religion and freedom of speech are part of our political traditions! Rather, the sins we commit result from failing to recognize the difference between faith and arrogance as we falsely assume that we have a God's-eye view of the truth and take it upon ourselves to condemn others. We assault the humanity of others when we attack them for not conforming to our own views of what is religiously appropriate or politically correct. We demean others when we view them as in some way inferior, when we subject them to ridicule and contempt, when we dismiss their ideas and concerns as unworthy of consideration, and when we fail to give recognition to their hopes and fears. The stage is set for the destruction of the humanity of others when we become preoccupied with "the cause," whatever it might be, and operate on the assumption that this cause is of such transcending importance that it sweeps all else before it.

The previous chapter noted that reason alone cannot provide final answers to ethical questions and that when all things are considered, we can only affirm the values to which we are committed as articles of faith. Faith, however, is not the top of the mountain—a point of vantage from which we can judge the whole world, condemning those who disagree with us. Faith, properly understood, points in the direction of ethics on the horizontal—an understanding of ethics that places us on the same level as everyone else—rather than ethics on the vertical, where we imagine that we are somehow on a higher level than others. Faith, properly understood, must begin with recognition of human finiteness. We are not God. Our knowledge, virtue, and power are not unlimited. To presume otherwise is to succumb to arrogance. To try to use God as a theological club with which to beat other people over the head is to misunderstand both the nature of God and what we can claim about God. In the final analysis, faith that is not born of humility is not really faith at all.

At the same time, faith is far more than humility. And it is far more than assent. There is a huge difference between faith and detached belief. Faith must have an impact on one's life if it is to be faith in the full sense of the term. If it does not, it is something other than faith. I might be able to say truthfully that I believe (or that I do not believe) that there is life in other solar systems without such a belief in any way having any impact on the way that I live my life. However, I cannot truthfully say that I am committed to justice and the affirmation of human dignity—or any other set of ideals—without allowing such an affirmation of faith to have an impact on what I do and how I relate to other people. In short, faith by its very nature compels action. Faith, properly understood, is action with humility. It is affirmation without arrogance. As noted in chapter 3, the prophet Micah got it right more than twenty-five centuries ago when he asked rhetorically, "And what does the Lord require of you but to do justice, and to love kindness, and to walk humbly with your God?" (Micah 6.8).

Ten Questions for Reflection and Discussion

1   What is the nature of faith?

2   Does one have to be religious in order to have faith?

3   Is faith inherently dangerous? If so, why? And in what ways?

4   Is it possible to view the world through the eyes of faith without succumbing to arrogance?

5   When does faith become arrogance?

6   To what extent, if at all, are we different from Tomás de Torquemada and John Calvin? To what extent, if at all, are we similar to them?

7   Is pride a sin? If so, in what ways do we commit the sin of pride?

8   Is it necessary to be religious in order to be moral?

9   Is it possible to be both religious and moral?

10   What is the nature of humility?

NOTES

1. Samuel Eliot Morison, *Admiral of the Ocean Sea: A Life of Christopher Columbus* (Boston: Little, Brown, 1942), 148.

2. William H. Prescott, *History of the Reign of Ferdinand and Isabella, the Catholic,* ed. Wilfred Harold Munro (Philadelphia: J. B. Lippincott, 1904), 3: 287.

3. Morison, *Admiral of the Ocean Sea,* 148.

4. *The Journal of Christopher Columbus (During His First Voyage, 1492–93) and Documents Relating to the Voyages of John Cabot and Caspar Corte Real,* trans. Clements R. Markham (New York: Burt Franklin, 1893), 17. See also John Stewart Collis, *Christopher Columbus* (New York: Stein & Day, 1977), 66.

5. Prescott, *Reign of Ferdinand and Isabella,* 296–300.

6. Edward Peters, *Inquisition* (New York: Free Press, 1988), 44.

7. Peters, *Inquisition,* 89–90.

8. Henry Kamen, *The Spanish Inquisition: A Historical Revision* (New Haven: Yale University Press, 1998), 88–90, 123–25, 160–63.

9. Rafael Sabatini, *Torquemada and the Spanish Inquisition: A History,* rev. ed. (Boston: Houghton Mifflin, 1924), 100–104.

10. Sabatini, *Torquemada,* 108.

11. Sabatini, *Torquemada,* 134, 138, 141–77.

12. Peters, *Inquisition,* 91. After 1500, the Edict of Grace was often replaced with an Edict of Faith threatening excommunication to all who failed to denounce heretics.

13. Peters, *Inquisition,* 92–93.

14. Peters, *Inquisition,* 92–93.

15. Peters, *Inquisition,* 94. See also Kamen, *Spanish Inquisition,* 177–96.

16. The Inquisition in Spain was officially ended by a decree issued July 15, 1834. (Kamen, *Spanish Inquisition,* 304).

17. Roland H. Bainton, *Hunted Heretic: The Life and Death of Michael Servetus* (Boston: Beacon Press, 1953), 3.

18. Carter Lindberg, *The European Reformations* (Oxford: Blackwell, 1996), 267–68. See also Steven Ozment, *The Age of Reform, 1250–1550: An Intellectual and Religious History of Late Medieval and Reformation Europe* (New Haven: Yale University Press, 1980), 369–70.

19. Lindberg, *European Reformations*, 268. See also Georgia Harkness, *John Calvin: The Man and His Ethics* (New York: Henry Holt, 1931), 40.

20. Ozment, *Age of Reform*, 370.

21. Quoted in Ozment, *Age of Reform*, 370.

22. Lindberg, *European Reformations*, 268.

23. Bainton, *Hunted Heretic*, 149–64.

24. Quoted by Harkness in *Calvin*, 42.

25. Quoted by Bainton in *Hunted Heretic*, 195.

26. Bainton, *Hunted Heretic*, 208.

27. Ozment, *Age of Reform*, 371.

28. Bainton, *Hunted Heretic*, 211–12.

29. Bainton, *Hunted Heretic*, 214.

30. The Servetus affair, it should be noted, was not the only occasion when religious dissenters lost their lives at the hands of Protestants. Among those dealt with harshly were the Anabaptists, who opposed infant baptism, believing that baptism should not be performed until a person was old enough to understand the nature of baptism and request it. Such being the case, the Anabaptists rebaptized adults who had been baptized as children, a practice that infuriated many of the leaders of the Protestant movement, including Zurich-based Ulrich Zwingli. In March of 1526, town magistrates, acting at Zwingli's behest, arrested three of the local leaders of the Anabaptist movement: George Blaurock, Conrad Grebel, and Felix Mantz. Owing to the "carelessness" of a prison guard, they escaped. Grebel died of the plague a few months later. Mantz and Blaurock were recaptured toward the end of the year and returned to Zurich, where rebaptism was now a capital offense punishable by drowning—a means of execution deliberately chosen as a parody of the Anabaptist belief in baptism by immersion. Since Blaurock was not a citizen of Zurich, he was whipped and run out of town, though his respite was only temporary, since he was executed three years later in Innsbruck. Mantz was executed in Zurich by drowning on January 5, 1527, the day he was condemned (Lindberg, *European Reformations*, 214–16; see also Ozment, *Age of Reform*, 328–32).

31. John Calvin, *Institutes of the Christian Religion*, trans. Ford Lewis Battles, ed. John T. McNeill (Philadelphia: Westminster Press, 1960), III, vii, 6.

32. Bainton, *Hunted Heretic*, 210.

33. Maurice Merleau-Ponty, "The Metaphysical in Man," in *Sense and*

Non-Sense, trans. Hubert L. Dreyfus and Patricia A. Dreyfus (Evanston, Ill.: Northwestern University Press, 1964), 95.

34. Reinhold Niebuhr, *Human Nature,* vol. 1 of *Nature and Destiny of Man* (New York: Charles Scribner's Sons, 1949), 188–203. Reinhold Niebuhr was H. Richard Niebuhr's older brother.

5

WHAT OUGHT TO COUNT ABOVE ALL ELSE?

—

More than two thousand years ago, Socrates (470?—399 B.C.E.) observed that "an unexamined life is not worth living."[1] Today, as in Socrates' time, a lot of folks shuffle through life without ever giving any serious thought to the question of what ought to count above all else. They go from class to class, from exam to exam, from the dining hall to their residence halls and back again. They attend planning meetings and sales strategy sessions, operate clanking machines and sophisticated computers, drive trucks that hum along our nation's highways and tractors that pull cultivators tilling the soil. They go to PTA meetings and band concerts, cocktail parties and football games, weddings and funerals. And then they die, their entire lives having slipped by without their ever having addressed in a serious way questions of meaning and purpose in life—questions that derive from, and are related to, the most fundamental questions of human existence.

Some try to avoid coming to grips with these fundamental questions of human existence by doing everything they can to make life one big party or otherwise opting for escapism. Escapism comes in many forms—living the life of a couch potato addicted to television, using mind-altering drugs, consuming alcohol for no purpose other than getting inebriated, having sex without commitment. Some try to give meaning and purpose to their lives by absolutizing the trivial or by exalting the insignificant. I once met a person who was preoccupied with collecting Mickey Mouse memorabilia. She had various incarnations of Mickey Mouse tucked away in just about every nook and cranny of her house, wore a Mickey Mouse wrist watch, and almost always wore clothing with some kind of Mickey Mouse insignia on it.

If it doesn't make any difference which house of morality we choose to inhabit, which faith we espouse, or which goals and objectives we identify as giving direction to our lives, living our lives for Mickey Mouse is probably just as good as anything else. Most of us, however, yearn for more. Most of us hope that when our days on earth have ended, the eulogies at our funerals and the epitaphs on our tombstones will say something more significant than "She lived her life for Mickey Mouse" or "He never really amounted to anything."

Some respond to this yearning for significance by striving for fame and fortune, in some cases achieving one or both. While there is much to be said for making the most of our God-given talents and abilities, simply striving for fame or fortune does little, if anything, to alleviate the feeling of hollowness that often accompanies the yearning for significance. Indeed, it is rather startling to discover how empty the lives of the rich and famous sometimes are. Would anyone really want to have swapped places with Howard Hughes, the eccentric billionaire who spent the last years of his life as a tormented recluse?[2] Or with Marilyn Monroe, the sex icon of the 1950s whose unhappy life was ended by a drug overdose?[3] Or with rock guitarist, singer, and songwriter Jimi Hendrix, who died of asphyxiation after taking an overdose of sleeping pills?[4] Or with legendary rock star Janis Joplin, an addict who, less than three weeks after Hendrix's tragic death, died an untimely death from an overdose of heroin?[5] Or with talented singer Karen Carpenter, who died at the age of thirty-two of complications from anorexia nervosa, a debilitating disorder that had tormented her for years?[6] Or with talented actor River Phoenix, who died of drug-induced heart failure while partying at a celebrity hangout?[7] Or with Kurt Cobain, the idol of Nirvana fans, who killed himself with a shotgun blast to the head?[8] The simple fact of the matter is that fame and fortune do not guarantee happiness or a sense of fulfillment.

I do not pretend to know whether the yearning for significance is something that is built into us from birth or something that is the result of cultural conditioning (though I suspect that there is some type of link with awareness of our mortality and anxieties related to dying). I am quite content to leave the matter of the origin of this yearning to psychologists, cultural anthropologists, and others engaged in the "nature vs. nurture" debate. But regardless of its origins, that yearning is there. And that's why questions of meaning and purpose in life end up being such important questions.

FORMATIVE EXPERIENCES

If what was noted in chapter 3 is correct (and quite obviously I believe that it is or I wouldn't have written it), we can't just think our way through these matters. To put this in slightly different language, reason alone can't determine what is good and right and proper and what ought to count above all else. That's why, as was suggested at the conclusion of chapter 3, the ultimate values that give form to our lives can only be asserted and affirmed as articles of faith.

But that is where things start getting a bit complicated. Unlike buying a car or a new coat, faith isn't something that we can just go out and acquire. Rather, there is an experiential dimension to faith. While, as will be noted in greater detail later in this chapter, we can choose to immerse ourselves in life-transforming experiences that change the way we view things, it is not apparent to me that we can just arbitrarily decide what to believe and what not to believe.

There is a delightful story that I first heard from one of my graduate school professors about a fellow by the name of Paddy O'Brien, who was a lifelong resident of County Cork in Ireland. Unfortunately, he developed a life-threatening disease of some sort. Shortly after his doctor gave him the unhappy news that it didn't look as if he would make it, Paddy astonished his family and friends by announcing that he had decided to become, of all things, a Presbyterian, a perspective that is not particularly popular in County Cork.

Paddy's parish priest (or, perhaps we should say, his former parish priest) decided that he'd better stop by and have a little talk with Paddy to see if the situation might be salvageable. "Paddy," the priest began, "you were baptized in this parish. You were confirmed in this parish. Both of your parents were lifelong Roman Catholics and are buried in the parish cemetery. All four of your grandparents were lifelong Roman Catholics and are buried in the parish cemetery. Indeed, six generations of O'Briens are buried in the parish cemetery. Whatever possessed you to up and decide to become a Presbyterian?"

"Ah, Father," Paddy replied, his voice weakened by his debilitating illness, "'tis far better that one of them dies than one of us."

Paddy O'Brien's conversion, it seems, was somewhat less than complete.

There is an underlying point here that is worth noting. Simply declaring that we are Presbyterians (or anything else) doesn't automatically make us Presbyterians (or anything else) in thought, word, or deed. Now it's within the range of the possible that if someone hangs out with Presbyterians long enough, whatever is involved in being a Presbyterian will rub off on him or her to the extent that he or she will start to think and act like a Presbyterian. To put this in slightly more formal language, in time the beliefs and values that give form to Presbyterianism will be assimilated and will come to be the faith that gives direction to that person's life. In the final analysis, there is a certain sense in which we don't just decide what beliefs and values should give form to our lives. Rather, the values that we espouse are, in substantial measure, the result of formative experiences that have been defining moments for us.

All of this might appear to be moving in the direction of some form of determinism—the view that we don't really freely choose what we believe or wish to do but rather that what we think and say and do is caused by environmental or genetic factors. That, however, is not what I am suggesting.

To be sure, some formative experiences are beyond our control. We did not choose the time or place of our birth, our parents, or the communities in which we spent our childhood years. We have encountered other formative experiences along the way. For those of us who were of draft age during the Vietnam era, the war in Vietnam forever changed the way that we view the world, as did the experiences of those who lived through the Great Depression of the 1930s and World War II. Similarly, serious illness, be it of a family member or illness that one experiences oneself, can have a tremendous impact on values and priorities. In the middle years of life, a former pastor of the church I attend was rushed off to Mayo Clinic in Rochester, Minnesota, for open-heart surgery. When he had recovered enough to reflect about his experience, he noted that when confronted with the possibility of his life slipping away, what once seemed important to him was no longer important and things he hadn't thought about all that much suddenly became very important. For him, as for many others, serious illness was a life-transforming experience.

But while some formative experiences just happen to us, others are the result of decisions we make. Going to college, for example, is often an eye-opening, horizon-broadening experience (which is why so many of us who teach for a living find sharing in the teaching-learning experience so delightful). For many students, college does more to foster personal growth and development, define career options, and shape the postcollege years than anything else they do. Because the nature of the educational opportunities and the environment at colleges and universities varies greatly, choosing a college or university to attend is one of the most important decisions that anyone can make.

There are other decisions as well that various individuals make, decisions that have a tremendous impact on their growth and development and help shape the sort of person they become. Stopping by the local Marine Corps recruiting office and signing up to serve in the military can bring one in contact with a range of experience that, one way or another, will change the way that one views the world. For those suffering from chemical dependency or other forms of addiction, voluntarily entering a therapy program can be a life-transforming experience. Working in a shelter for abused children or for a hunger-relief agency can result in changed perceptions and redefined values. So also can many other job experiences and activities in which participation is voluntary.

Not everyone, of course, responds the same way to a particular type of experience. Students attending the same college and taking exactly the same courses sometimes come out of the experience with very different perspectives and very different sets of values. The same is true with respect to those serving in the military and those who share many other experiences. The perspectives that emerge and the values that are affirmed are the result of the interaction between what is brought to the situation and what is experienced. And since different individuals bring different things to what otherwise are common experiences, the outcome often differs from person to person.

There is a certain sense, it might be added, in which the faiths we affirm and the values to which they give expression are always works in progress. If the values that give direction to our lives are, at least in part, the result of various experiences that have given form to our lives, it stands to reason that there often is reevaluation and reformulation of values as the situations in which we find ourselves change.[9] For example, it is not unusual for people to change their political views in the middle years of life when they have college-bound children to support and mortgages to pay. (Some of us are even to be found among that number!)

It should also be noted that when choosing to immerse ourselves in experiences of various types, we seldom, if ever, are able to anticipate fully what the impact of these experiences will be. We seldom, if ever, know exactly where the roads we choose to travel will take us or how the experiences we encounter will shape the sort of person that we are and give definition to the values that inform the decisions we make. At the same time, it is possible to have at least some sense of what the lay of the land is when we come to a fork in the road and choose one course of action in preference to another. For example, it is probably a safe bet that working as a volunteer in an after-school reading program for disadvantaged children is likely to have a far different impact on one than working in a chop shop grinding serial numbers off stolen BMWs and Toyotas.

What ought to count above all else? If we are not satisfied with wandering around aimlessly, how might we go about becoming involved in life-transforming experiences that give greater depth and meaning to our lives? And what might those experiences be? To these matters we now turn.

DISCOVERING THE PERSON IN OTHERS

There is considerable irony in the fact that the best way to discover greater depth and meaning in our own lives is to forget about ourselves and start paying more attention to other people. The nature of this dynamic is reflected in a beautiful old prayer attributed to St. Francis of Assisi that reads, in part:

Lord, make us instruments of your peace . . .
Grant that we may not so much seek
to be consoled as to console;
to be understood as to understand;
to be loved as to love.
For it is in giving that we receive.[10]

Many of us are so preoccupied with our own anxieties and insecurities that we pay very little attention to other people. When we do take note of others, we often view them exclusively in functional terms—as accountants or actuaries, farmers or factory workers, mechanics or merchants, physicians or pharmacists. Sometimes we see others as nothing more than means to be used in accomplishing our own goals and objectives. We totally ignore Kant's advice, "So act that you use humanity, whether in your own person or in the person of any other, always at the same time as an end, never merely as a means."[11] Sometimes we go a step further and view others simply as problems with which we have to deal, lumping them together in depersonalized groups—labor, management, shareholders, Republicans, Democrats, bureaucrats, students, faculty, administrators, sororities, fraternities, and various other assorted groups of individuals we view as "troublemakers." And sometimes we simply ignore others. At a conference I attended, a seminary student recounted how he had been so preoccupied with the causes to which he was committed that he was oblivious to the fact that the person living right across the hall from him was grieving greatly as his mother was dying from cancer. Many of us are often like that seminary student.

Some of the most wonderful experiences I have ever had happened while I was doing research for a book I wrote on intergenerational issues.[12] For a number of years, I had been strongly influenced by the ideas of Reinhold Niebuhr, who suggested that the best that we can do to ensure a greater measure of social justice is to confront power with power. In a frequently quoted passage, he asserts, "Conflict is inevitable, and in this conflict power must be challenged with power."[13]

As I worked on intergenerational issues, however, I realized that if challenging power with power is the best that we can do, we are stuck with injustice when it comes to intergenerational issues since the very young and very old possess very little power. Not wanting to abandon all hope of achieving a greater measure of intergenerational justice, I began to explore other approaches. It occurred to me that the key to justice might be found, not in power relationships, but in awareness of, and sensitivity to, the personhood of others. That is where the ethics of listening started coming into the picture. Deciding that I ought to practice what I was preaching, I interviewed individuals from different age groups and from diverse socioeconomic backgrounds, making every effort to be as open-minded as possible as I listened to their life stories. Some were people I had known for years—or at least thought I had known for years, though I must confess that when I sat down and listened to what they had to say, I discovered that I hadn't always been tuned in to where they were coming from. Others were individuals I met at various events. Friends and colleagues who knew that I was working on the project brought others to my attention.

It was an eye-opening experience! The individuals whose life stories I heard included a retired college president who sadly characterized the twentieth century (more than nine decades of which he had experienced) as "a century of nothing but war." A delightful centenarian reminisced about the passage of the Nineteenth Amendment, recalling, "We marched and we marched right in front of those men!" A survivor of the Japanese attack on Pearl Harbor, who lost a brother on the *Arizona,* said of the carnage, "It was a terrible, frightening sight to see." Another veteran of the war spoke of the nightmares he continues to experience, even though he tries not to think about the war. A Mexican American grandmother recalled the discrimination to which she had been subjected and expressed gratitude that her grandchildren have things better, adding, "I am not hateful." An African American teacher told of the barriers she encountered when trying to find a teaching job and said of her students, "Unlike us, they will not be denied!" A former Peace Corps volunteer who now works as an editor said of life today, "Everything is so hurried." A baby boomer lamented, "It's so hard to find security and stability." A former flower child recalled, "We were into small acts of kindness." A wheelchair-bound victim of multiple sclerosis spoke of the challenges he faces but added, "God didn't bring us this far to leave us." A friend of his, who had recently been released from prison after having been incarcerated for homicide, spoke with great sadness and regret about what he had done. "I know that I can't bring that guy back. I took a life; now I want to give something back." A graduate student who is a lesbian grieved the ending of a long-term relationship and talked about her struggle with questions of identity and gender roles. A welfare mother nearing the completion of her college education observed, "I hope to find a job that will support my daughter the way I want to support her." A young Ácoma Pueblo mother spoke of her effort to maintain the tribal traditions for her daughter while providing for her economically. A junior high school student noted in an essay for which he received an award at a Martin Luther King Day celebration, "As I walk down the street this day, my heart fills with sorrow." He observed that if Martin Luther King "could see us now, tears would drop from his eyes."[14]

If listening is to be a mode of discovery, we must be open-minded about what others have to say, particularly when they give expression to views at odds with those we hold. When we filter everything through our own beliefs and preconceptions, we miss out on much of what is being said. And we risk significantly misconstruing what we do hear. Preconceptions often result in misperceptions.

Being open-minded listeners, it should be added, in no way means that we ought to suspend all judgment about what others say and do, thereby opting for an oversimplified "I'm okay, you're okay" mind-set that in effect says that whatever anyone is inclined to say or do is just fine. Nor does it suggest that we should never give expression to our own views when engaged in conversations with others or in any way disagree with what they say. Rather, being open-minded simply means that when we are in the listening phase of the communication process, we need to set aside temporarily our own beliefs and views so that we can better hear what is being said. It also means that when others say and do things at odds with values we hold dear, we ought to do our best to see the person behind what we perceive to be their faults, rather than simply focus on the things that we believe they are doing wrong.

None of this is easy to accomplish. It is far easier to lead with our own views and preconceptions—to judge first and then try to make it appear as if we are listening, even though the reality is otherwise. The simple fact of the matter, however, is that temporarily setting aside our own views and judgments is precisely what must be done if we are to be careful, open-minded listeners—if we are to prevent preconceptions from becoming misperceptions.

There is a particular sense of forgiveness that comes into play here, a sense of forgiveness that contrasts sharply with the way that forgiveness is often understood. Forgiveness is often envisioned as a big eraser that comes down from the heavens and wipes from the blackboard of life the check marks after our names, the result being that we no longer have to pay the penalties for the things we have done wrong. That's not what is at stake here. Rather, the sense of forgiveness that is operative here is the ability to see the person behind what we perceive to be his or her faults, while in no way suggesting that those who have done things that are wrong should be excused from assuming responsibility for what they have done.

One of the most insightful (and least noted) biblical passages tells of Jesus having dinner with tax collectors and other sinners:

> And as he sat at dinner in the house, many tax collectors and sinners came and were sitting with him and his disciples. When the Pharisees

saw this, they said to his disciples, "Why does your teacher eat with tax collectors and sinners?" But when he heard this, he said, "Those who are well have no need of a physician, but those who are sick. Go and learn what this means, 'I desire mercy, not sacrifice.' For I have come to call not the righteous but sinners." (Matthew 9.10–13)

The tax collectors of Jesus' day were notorious crooks who cheated taxpayers by charging them more than they owed and cheated the government by skimming off part of the take.[15] Yet, here was Jesus having dinner with them! The religious types were aghast! Didn't Jesus realize what he was doing?

Jesus, of course, was in no way condoning cheating or any of the other terrible things the crooked tax collectors were doing. And when it came time for Jesus to pay whatever taxes carpenters and itinerant teachers paid in those days, I seriously doubt that Jesus said, "I don't mind being cheated. Help yourself. Take whatever you want."[16]

That, however, is not the point of the story. Rather, the story serves to remind us that Jesus was able to see something most of us fail to see—the person behind the faults. While not excusing their conduct, Jesus realized that even crooked tax collectors are human beings worthy of our compassion and understanding.

The people most of us meet in day-to-day life have flaws of character of far lesser magnitude than the crooked tax collectors of Jesus' time. Yet we often magnify what we perceive to be their faults, making mountains of things that are trivial. By so doing, we block out any possibility of seeing the humanity of others. When we start criticizing other people for this and that, for wrongs that we perceive or imagine, it is very easy to overlook the fact that those with whom we share life on planet Earth are real people just like ourselves. People who have hopes and fears, moments of joy and moments of sorrow, times of success and times of failure.

There is a certain practical sense in which becoming aware of the humanity of others changes the sort of person that we are. The widely read Jewish philosopher Martin Buber (1878–1965) was aware of this transformation of the self when he distinguished between the "I-Thou" relationship and the "I-It" relationship, the former being an interpersonal relationship while the latter is essentially nothing more than that of a subject acting on an object. He suggested that "the I of the primary word I-Thou is a different I from that of the primary word I-It."[17] (Buber referred to I-Thou and I-It as "primary words" that are "not isolated words, but combined words.")[18] There's something to that. The experience of intersubjectivity—that is, the experience of relating to others as persons, not simply as objects—brings with it a different type of consciousness and awareness. When the humanity of others registers on our consciousness, the ethical framework within which we operate is redefined and restructured. And in the process, we become different sorts of persons.

CHARITY

A few years ago, a student stopped by my office bubbling with enthusiasm about an experience she had with Generations, a program introduced by campus ministry to help bridge generation gaps. As part of this program, she was regularly visiting a resident of an area nursing home. "I thought I was helping Margaret," the student exclaimed, "but it's amazing how much she has been helping me!" She had discovered the nature of charity.

When we hear the word "charity," we often think about giving money to those who are less fortunate—for example, donating money to the local food pantry or to the Salvation Army. Helping those who are less fortunate is an important part of charity. But it is only a small part of what charity entails. Charity, in its fullest sense, involves living in and experiencing community. It is discovering the humanity of others—and our own humanity in the process. It is understanding others and being understood.

The English word "charity" comes from the Old French word *charité*, which carried with it the notions of fondness, affection, and valuing greatly—connotations that are today often associated with the English word "cherish." Also of etymological significance is the Latin word *caritas*, which was often used to translate the Greek word *agape*, found both in the love commandment ("You shall love your neighbor as yourself") and the apostle Paul's reference to faith, hope and love in 1 Corinthians 13. Caritas was often defined as "dearness, love founded on esteem."[19] The Greek verb from which agape is derived is customarily defined as "to treat with affection" and "to regard with brotherly love," as when treating a stranger as if he or she were a member of the family. Ancient Greeks, it might be added, did not use the term agape to refer to giving money to those less fortunate; rather, they used the term *eleemosyne*, from which the English word "alms" is derived. Eleemosyne involved pity, which agape did not.[20]

We all need and desire charity. This is not to suggest, of course, that everyone should be getting food stamps regardless of income level. Rather, it is to suggest that we all have a need to be taken seriously, to be treated with respect and esteem, and to be understood—in short, to be treated in a charitable manner. "They just don't get it" is the recurring lament of frustrated teenagers, alienated spouses, and others pained by the brokenness of relationships of many different sorts.

Charity involves more than simply being charitable in our relations with others. As the student involved in Generations discovered, when we take time to listen to others and give recognition to their humanity, our own lives are enriched in the process. There is a good deal of wisdom to be found in the beautiful old prayer attributed to St. Francis of Assisi to which reference was made earlier in this chapter. In many cases, when we seek understanding just for the sake of being understood, love just for the sake of being loved, and consolation just for the sake of being consoled, the result is failure and frustration. As the insightful centuries-old prayer reminds us, it is as we extend understanding to others that, in many cases, others come to better understand us—and that we come to better understand ourselves. And similarly with being loved and consoled, for, as the prayer attributed to St. Francis of Assisi reminds us, "it is in giving that we receive."

NOT THE MOUNTAIN ABOVE, BUT IN THE VALLEY BELOW

For reasons that were noted in chapters 3 and 4, we would be well advised to disabuse ourselves of the illusion that we can make it to the top of the mountain, whether by dint of reason or by faith. Our finiteness is such that there is no place on which we can stand and judge the whole world. "Mountaintop morality" is invariably mistaken morality, at least in its form and structure, if not in its content. Rather, the nature and substance of morality are best discovered on a horizontal plane—on the plain in the valley below as we live and experience interpersonal relationships that recognize and affirm the humanity of all of our fellow human beings. The harsh moralizing that typically accompanies mountaintop morality, whether from the left, the right, or somewhere in between, often gets in the way of the interpersonal relationships that are necessary if we are to recognize fully and affirm the personhood of others—and of ourselves.

In this chapter, relatively little has been said about God. In part, that's because the nature of God far exceeds what any of us are capable of understanding. We can only use metaphorical language such as "God is love" to try to conceptualize what God might be like. There is another reason as well for being sparing in our use of religious language. Religious language, which strikes many as pompous and harshly judgmental, sometimes gets in the way of ethics. It also runs the risk of overlooking the fact that there are a lot of good, decent, kind, gentle people who don't have any religious bones in their bodies. The simple fact of the matter is that one doesn't have to be religious to be ethical or to recognize and respond to the humanity of our fellow human beings.

At the same time, religious traditions, including various expressions of Jewish, Christian, and Islamic traditions, are rich in ethical content. There is much to be gained by studying these and other religious traditions. Religion is a rich source to draw upon when addressing ethical issues. But it is not the only well from which water can be drawn.

While in no way insisting that one must be religious in order to be ethical, I also firmly believe that God, who far exceeds anything we can comprehend, touches our lives in a multitude of ways—including ways that often lie beyond the limits of our comprehension and awareness. God is present in the stillness of quiet times of contemplation and meditation. (In our busy lives, we often overlook the importance of times of stillness.) God touches our lives through those whose lives intersect with ours as we travel along the roads that crisscross the verdant valley in which we live—friends, neighbors, teachers, and many others, including the destitute and those who are sick, and outcasts and those who are often overlooked. God is present in the lives of people who are entirely unaware of that presence. I am reminded of a remark William Sloan Coffin made a number of years ago in a sermon preached in Battell Chapel at Yale University: "Young people today might not believe in God, but God still believes in them!" What was true in the 1960s is true today as well. God still believes in people, young and old, and is present in their acts of kindness and compassion.

ADDING QUALITY TO OUR LIVES

What ought to count above all else? If we are not satisfied with wandering around aimlessly, how might we go about finding greater meaning and purpose in lives? How might we add quality and a sense of fulfillment to our lives? While there's nothing at all wrong with enjoying a new car or the latest CD, piling up material possessions does little, if anything, to add quality to our lives. The nature of the interpersonal relationships that we experience has far more to do with our quality of life than our level of affluence. How might we discover and experience greater meaning and purpose in our lives while improving the quality of the interpersonal relationships that we experience? By listening carefully and respectfully to what others have to say, particularly when they disagree with us. By being aware of, and responsive to, the fears and anxieties of others instead of being preoccupied with our own fears and anxieties. By using our talents and abilities in life-enhancing and life-serving ways within the context of caring community. And by being a neighbor to both our near and our distant neighbors, for in rediscovering the humanity of others, we rediscover our own humanity.

In days that are now part of the distant past, parish pastors, parents, and others in positions of authority often tried to scare folks into walking the straight and narrow by painting terrifying pictures of the fires of hell awaiting the wicked. But in an era in which otherworldly images of hell have, in substantial measure, disappeared from our consciousness, that no longer works. If concerns about avoiding eternal damnation are no longer part of our consciousness, why, if at all, should we be affirmative of, and responsive to, the humanity of our fellow human beings? Some might respond by saying that we ought to do so because that is what the Lord and Giver of Life wants us to do—a perfectly plausible and coherent response when viewed from an explicitly religious perspective. There is another reason as well that legislates in favor of a morality based on respect for persons within the context of caring community. As Aristotle, Aquinas, and others have recognized throughout the ages, we ought to be moral, not only because so doing contributes to the well-being of others, but also because so doing contributes to our own well-being as we more fully realize our own humanity. To be human and realize it is one of the most wonderful things that can happen to anyone.

Ten Questions for Reflection and Discussion

1   What do you believe ought to count above all else?

2   How important do you believe fame and fortune are?

3   What experiences have been formative for you?

4   In what ways, if at all, would you like to change the sort of person that you are?

5   How might you go about changing the sort of person you are, if so doing is desirable?

6   How might we improve our listening skills?

7   Is it possible to be a nonjudgmental listener while disagreeing with what others believe and do?

8   As you see things, what does forgiveness involve?

9   How might we become more forgiving of others?

10 In what ways, if at all, does God touch our lives through the lives of other people?

NOTES

1. Plato, *Apology,* in *Euthyphro, Apology, Crito,* trans. F. J. Church and Robert D. Cumming, 2d ed. (Indianapolis: Bobbs-Merrill, 1956), 45 (XXVI-II, 38). Socrates' trial provides the setting for this statement. By a vote of 281 to 220, the Athenian court has convicted Socrates of "corrupting the young"—the alleged corruption apparently coming in the form of causing them to think for themselves. The question of what the punishment should be has not yet been resolved. Some of Socrates' friends suggest that he should indicate willingness to accept exile. That, however, does not meet with Socrates' approval. He states, "It is the most difficult thing in the world to make you understand why I cannot do that. . . . And if I tell you that no greater good can happen to a man than to discuss human excellence every day and the other matters about which you have heard me arguing and examining myself and others, and that an unexamined life is not worth living, then you will believe me still less." And so the Athenian court, by an even greater margin than in the original decision, sentences Socrates to death.

2. John A. Garraty and Mark C. Games, eds., *American National Biography* (New York: Oxford University Press, 1999), 11: 524–26.

3. Garraty and Games, *American National Biography,* 15: 684–86. Though originally ruled a suicide, some believe that Monroe's death resulted from an accidental overdose of drugs prescribed by her physician.

4. Garraty and Games, *American National Biography,* 10: 588–89.

5. Garraty and Games, *American National Biography,* 12: 262–64.

6. Garraty and Games, *American National Biography,* 4: 430–31.

7. "River Phoenix, 23, Intense Young Actor in a Range of Films," *New York Times,* 1 November 1993, D9; and Seth Mydans, "Death of River Phoenix Is Linked to Use of Cocaine and Morphine," *New York Times,* 13 November 1993, 8. The coroner ruled that Phoenix died from "acute multiple drug intoxication."

8. Timothy Egan, "Kurt Cobain, Hesitant Poet of 'Grunge Rock,' Dead at 27," *New York Times,* 9 April 1994, 1. See also Jon Pareles, "Reflections on Cobain's Short Life," *New York Times,* 11 April 1994, C11.

9. See, e.g., Erik H. Erikson, *The Life Cycle Completed: A Review* (New York: Norton, 1982), 55–82.

10. Included in *Lutheran Book of Worship* (Minneapolis: Augsburg, 1978), 48.

11. Immanuel Kant, *Groundwork of the Metaphysics of Morals,* trans. and ed. Mary Gregor (Cambridge: Cambridge University Press, 1996), 38 (4:429).

12. Daniel E. Lee, *Generations and the Challenge of Justice* (Lanham, Md.: University Press of America, 1996).

13. Reinhold Niebuhr, *Moral Man and Immoral Society* (New York: Charles Scribner's Sons, 1960), xv.

14. Lee, *Generations,* 38–45, 64–74, 110–14, 116–19, 128–30, 140–44, 148–50, 158–65, 168–70.

15. The Romans did not have a highly developed civil service system. Rather, much of what is typically done by government agencies today, including the collection of taxes, was often contracted out to the highest bidder. As a result, much of the tax collecting was done by private individuals known as *publicani* (publicans). Though complaints of abuse were frequent, Roman officials often found it more profitable to allow the abuses to continue, rather than take steps to curtail the exploitation of those living in the provinces (Simon Hornblower and Antony Spawforth, eds., *The Oxford Classical Dictionary,* 3d ed. [Oxford: Oxford University Press, 1996], 1275–76). During Jesus' time, the power (and abuses) of publicani extended far beyond collecting taxes, for they also often functioned as brokers controlling access to markets and the prices for various commodities. Many did not hesitate to use their power for their own enrichment. Not surprisingly, they were intensely disliked by those struggling to make a living. Some scholars believe that Matthew (Levi), whose office was located in Capernaum, was a broker (perhaps *the* broker) for the fishing industry in that area (K. C. Hanson and Douglas E. Oakman, *Palestine in the Time of Jesus* [Minneapolis: Fortress Press, 1998], 106–7, 113–16).

16. Was Jesus a taxpayer? While tax records dating back to Jesus' time are hard to come by, it is likely that Jesus did pay taxes. After the replacement of Archelaus with direct Roman rule of Judea and Samaria in 6 C.E. the Roman tax system was extended to these provinces. This included the *tributum capitis,* a head tax on each person. The tributum capitis was probably also collected in Galilee, where Jesus lived. The tax is believed to have been one denarius (a silver Roman coin which, during Jesus' adult years, featured the head of Tiberius Caesar on one side) for men of the ages fourteen to forty-five. A denarius was the wage typically paid a laborer for a full day's work (John J.

Rousseau and Rami Arav, *Jesus and His World: An Archaeological and Cultural Dictionary* [Minneapolis: Fortress Press, 1995], 55–61, 275–79). The tributum capitis plays a role in the story found in all three of the Synoptic Gospels in which Jesus is asked whether it is lawful to pay taxes to the emperor. Jesus responds by asking his questioners to show him one of the coins used for the tax. One of them produces a denarius. Jesus asks whose image is on the coin. When they answer that it is that of the emperor, Jesus responds, "'Give therefore to the emperor the things that are the emperor's and to God the things that are God's'" (Matt. 22.15–22, Mark 12.13–17, and Luke 20.20–26). The tributum capitis was by no means the only tax that those living in Galilee and Judea paid during Jesus' time. Along with taxes levied on virtually all stages of production, including, in all probability, the items produced by carpenters, all Jewish males were required to pay an annual half-shekel temple tax. (A shekel was a Hebrew coin equivalent to four denarii.) Even though the amount of the temple tax was stated in terms of traditional Hebrew coinage, temple authorities expected it to be paid with coins minted by the Phoenician city of Tyre. The Tyrian didrachma was the equivalent of a half-shekel, while the Tyrian tetradrachma, which featured the head of the Tyrian god Melkart, was the equivalent of the shekel. In preferring Tyrian coins with images of Phoenician gods, temple authorities apparently put practicality ahead of religious purity. With the Jewish population subject to the temple tax estimated at two million, the temple tax, if collected from all Jews subject to taxation, would have amounted to the equivalent of 14.5 tons of silver every year—a tidy amount even when measured by today's standards (Rousseau and Arav, *Jesus and His World*, 55–57). Matthew 17 includes a story that begins with the collectors of the temple tax asking Peter whether Jesus pays the temple tax. Peter assures them that Jesus does but, when he catches up with Jesus later in the day, decides he'd better check it out with Jesus. After noting that the children of kings are usually not taxed, Jesus instructs Peter, "'However, so that we do not give offense to them, go to the sea and cast a hook; take the first fish that comes up; and when you open its mouth, you will find a coin; take that and give it to them for you and me.'" To the dismay of many generations of taxpayers who fish, the author of Matthew does not say what species of fish it would be. Tradition has it that the fish was what is popularly known today as "Saint Peter's Fish" *(Tilapia galilea),* a fish that feeds on plankton. However, since *Tilapia galilea* is a surface fish typically caught using nets, it is more likely that the fish to which reference was made was either a *Barbus longiceps* or a *Barbus canis,* both of which are bottom feeders that might have scooped up a coin. Since nets don't work very well when attempting to catch bottom feeders, this type of fish is usually caught with baited hooks attached to lines. During Jesus' time, fishing lines were usually made of fibers from the stem of the flax plant, the same plant from which linen is made (Rousseau and Arav, *Jesus and His World,* 94–95).

17. Martin Buber, *I and Thou,* trans. Ronald Gregor Smith, 2d ed. (New York: Charles Scribner's Sons, 1958), 3. The German title of *I and Thou* (the volume was first published in Germany in 1923) is *Ich und Du.* As those familiar with the German language know, du is the familiar form of the second-person singular pronoun. The use of du in the title, rather than the more formal Sie, serves to underscore the personal dimension of the I-Thou relationship.

18. Buber, *I and Thou,* 3.

19. *Oxford English Dictionary,* 2d ed., s.v. "charity." In the 1881 Revised Standard Version of the Bible and in subsequent versions based on this translation, agape has been uniformly translated as "love." Thus, for example, the RSV translation of 1 Cor. 13.13 makes reference to "faith, hope, love," rather than, as in some older translations, "faith, hope, charity."

20. *An Intermediate Greek-English Lexicon,* based on the 7th ed. of Henry George Liddell and Robert Scott's *Greek-English Lexicon* (Oxford: Clarendon Press, 1961), 4, 248. I am indebted to my friend and colleague Thomas R. Banks, professor of classics at Augustana College, for elucidating the historical usage of agape among ancient Greeks. See also Lee, *Generations,* 9–11, 245–49.

6

IS A PUBLIC MORALITY POSSIBLE?

—

One of my graduate school professors enjoyed telling a story about three members of the clergy—a rabbi, a Roman Catholic priest, and a Protestant minister—who got together to discuss some issue in ethics. The rabbi prefaced his remarks by saying, "According to tradition, this is what ought to be done." The priest began by saying, "According to the church, this is what ought to be done." The Protestant minister simply leaned back in his chair and said, "Well, in my opinion, this is what ought to be done."

Like most caricatures, the anecdote is somewhat misleading. Many Protestants, for example, would preface their remarks by saying, "According to the Bible, this is what ought to be done." One doesn't have to read very far in the writings of Calvin or most other Protestant theologians to find biblical quotations cited to lend support to the positions that are taken. At the same time, as in many caricatures, there is also an element of truth in the story that my graduate school professor delighted in telling. There *is* a strong streak of individualism in Protestant thought. Historically, many Protestants have believed that it is the faith of the individual that is of paramount significance. And about that, they are right.

Like Archimedes of old, we might long for a place on which to stand so that we can move the whole world. There is no such place to be found. All that we can do is ground the value claims that we make in the confessions of faith that give form to our lives—confessions that must, if realism is to be maintained, begin with a statement of humility that acknowledges human finiteness.

In chapter 1, the question of why, if at all, we should comply with the law was raised. The chapter concluded by noting that whatever obligation there is to comply with the law derives from morality, not from the mere existence of law. Though Thoreau oversimplified things a bit in his essay on civil disobedience, he was pretty close to being right when he stated that "the only obligation which I have a right to assume, is to do at any time what I think is right."[1] The deeply held beliefs that give form to our lives and are given expression in the faiths that we confess, be they religious or secular in nature, are the reference points—indeed the only reference points—that define our obligations. It is these beliefs and value affirmations that bind us in conscience.

The word "obligation" comes from the Latin word *ligare*, which means "to bind. " (Ligare also provides the etymological roots for other English words such as "ligament," the tough tissue that holds joints together, and, according to some scholars, "religion.")[2] In a very literal sense, to be obligated is to be bound to do something. The relationship between faith and obligation is reflected in the statement one often hears when someone says that he or she is "bound in conscience" to do something. In its most basic sense, obligation is being bound to act in a certain way by the ideals to which we are committed. For example, if we are serious about affirming human dignity, there are certain things, such as ridiculing others or maliciously destroying their property, that we just can't do. Similarly, if we take seriously the notion of love for our neighbors, the very nature of this ethical ideal demands that we be sensitive to the needs and concerns of others. In short, we are bound in conscience by the ideals that we affirm—ideals that give form and substance to the ways of life that we live.

MORAL COMMUNITY

But what about others? If the obligations that we have derive from the values that we affirm, is there any meaningful way in which we can argue that others have obligations? Any way that goes beyond simply saying, "In my opinion, this is what you ought to be doing"?

The value affirmations that we make do not bind others in conscience. One person's faith is never a sufficient basis for another person's condemnation. If the claims of obligation we make pertaining to other individuals are to be anything more than statements of opinion about what they ought to be doing, these claims must derive from values that give form to their lives. Other people can be bound in conscience only by the values they hold dear, not by the affirmations of faith we make.

It is unlikely, of course, that we would call upon others to do things at odds with values we hold dear. For example, suppose that someone claims to be a dedicated bank robber but never gets around to robbing any banks. Those of us with deep moral reservations about bank robbery would probably not say to the self-professed bank robber, "You claim to be a bank robber but never rob any banks. You really ought to make good on the values that you affirm by getting your act put together and robbing a few banks. You cannot in good conscience do otherwise."

As this somewhat facetious hypothetical example illustrates, we are likely to appeal to values other people affirm only if they are consistent with values we affirm. Thus it is only within the context of *moral community*—here defined as two or more people who maintain a continuing commitment to common values—that claims of obligation pertaining to other people make sense.

Sometimes a particular moral community encompasses an entire way of life, as, for instance, monastic communities in which all members affirm the same values and follow the same routines. In other cases, moral community is partial or fragmentary. In these situations, those making up the moral community have some values in common but disagree about other matters. Moral community, it might be added, admits of working coalitions as well as all-encompassing common values. For example, some might support a particular school referendum because they are concerned about the quality of education their children are receiving, while others support the referendum because they believe that improving schools will enhance real estate values. But even though motivating reasons might differ and there might not be moral community on more abstract levels, there is still moral community with respect to the question of whether the referendum should be approved. And regardless of the reasons that various members of the community have for supporting the referendum, there is a basis for saying that they have an obligation to go to the polls and vote for it. In short, whether moral community is all-encompassing or partial, vertically integrated or present only in the form of working coalitions, the umbrella of moral community only needs to be large enough to cover the act in question in order to enable making claims of obligation pertaining to others.[3]

In some cases—many monastic communities, for example—identifying moral community is an easy task. But in pluralistic societies such as the one in which we live, finding common values is far more problematic. Indeed, the very nature of pluralism is such that one should not expect to find complete moral community.

The presence of ethical pluralism, however, should not lead us to abandon all hope of finding common values. Even though those with whom we rub shoulders might differ from us in many ways, that does not mean that we don't have anything in common. Moreover, as already noted, moral community need not be a complete way of life in order to be useful. It only needs to be broad enough to encompass values related to the act in question.

All too often, we focus on that which separates us rather than on what we have in common with other people. As was noted in the previous chapter, we often find it much easier to be judgmental than to be understanding of where others are coming from. The umbrella of moral community can often be more fully extended if we develop our listening skills and expand our horizons by doing everything we can to be more understanding of others.

In other cases, new umbrellas of understanding can be opened by focusing on the particular and on the practical rather than on more abstract considerations. Stephen Toulmin, who served on the National Commission for the Protection of Human Subjects of Biomedical and Behavioral Research, observed that when the commission considered specific cases, there was often consensus. But when the discussion moved to justifying principles and other more abstract considerations, disagreement was far more frequent.[4]

Philosopher Richard T. DeGeorge makes a distinction between *radical moral pluralism* and *pluralism of moral principles*. Radical moral pluralism involves completely different sets of values with no possibility for agreement. In contrast, pluralism of moral principles allows agreement on some levels under some circumstances. He writes:

A plurality of moral principles within a society does not necessarily mean irreconcilable diversity. Pluralism on the level of moral principles is compatible with social agreement on the morality of many basic practices. Such agreement does not necessarily involve agreement on the moral principles that different people use to evaluate practices. The vast majority of the members of our society, for instance, agree that murder is wrong. Some members of our society operate at the level of conventional morality and do not ask why murder is wrong. Some may believe it is wrong because the God in whom they believe forbids such acts; others because it violates human dignity; still others because murder has serious consequences for society as a whole; and so on.[5]

When radical moral pluralism is present, possibilities for moral community do not exist. But when the pluralism is pluralism of moral principles, it is often possible to identify moral community on some level. Or if moral community sufficient to encompass the issue or issues in question is not immediately apparent, measures can sometimes be taken to broaden the reach of moral community. Whether accomplished by being a careful listener or by building working coalitions, broadening the reach of the umbrella of moral community extends the range of moral discourse. This enables discussions of moral issues set against the backdrop of common values, rather than encounters that degenerate into shouting matches as words (and sometimes other things as well) are hurled back and forth with no semblance of civility. Even when disagreement persists, as it sometimes does since human perception and understanding are not infallible, discussions within the context of moral community almost always carry with them a greater degree of civility.

FOSTERING MORAL COMMUNITY

In practice, being a careful listener simply involves discovering moral community that already exists. But what about fostering moral community by building new moral communities? In a pluralistic society, of course, this means that someone has to change his or her mind, adopting, at least in part, a different set of values.

We should not automatically assume that when efforts are made to sort out differences and establish moral community, those who disagree with us are the ones who ought to change their minds. We would all do well to pause from time to time and ask ourselves if our own value priorities are right. A little introspection never hurts. In fact, sometimes it does a lot of good, bringing us to our senses and causing us to reorder our priorities. At the same time, deeply held beliefs that bind us in conscience are not likely to be changed by a little introspection. Nor should they be changed if we devoutly believe that they are good and right and proper. In these situations, attention invariably shifts to others as hope is expressed that they will change their views so that moral community can be established.

There is nothing inherently wrong with encouraging others to adopt values that one believes to be good and right and proper. We would be well advised to remember, however, that going around preaching morality is almost always the wrong way to try to build moral community. In many cases, being too "preachy" or wearing one's religion on one's sleeve ends up being counterproductive. William Diehl, a former manager of sales at Bethlehem Steel Corporation, recalls a supervisor who asked anyone with a problem to join him in his glass-enclosed office. He would then close the door (though anyone who wished to do so could still see through the glass walls), read from the Bible he always kept on his desk, bow his head and, with the person with the problem sitting by his desk, pray for that person. The practical result of this very public display of piety was that anyone with a problem of any sort did everything possible to make certain the supervisor didn't find out about it.[6]

In the previous chapter, it was noted that we can, at least in part, change the sort of person that we are by voluntarily participating in life-transforming experiences. In like manner, we can, in some instances and to some extent, have an impact on the life-transforming experiences that give form to the lives of other people. The type of home that parents provide for their children is an obvious example of this. And though those of us professionally involved in education sometimes overestimate the significance of what we are doing, there is a very real sense in which we are involved in creating life-forming and -transforming experiences for the students in our classes.

BOTH LOVE AND LIMITS

In response to growing concern about school violence, some have advocated posting the Ten Commandments in school classrooms. Apart from raising some rather sticky church-state issues, posting the Ten Commandments on school bulletin boards probably wouldn't hurt anything.[7] However, those who advocate so doing are naïve if they think that posting the Ten Commandments will solve the problem of violence or any of the other problems afflicting our schools. The process of value formation is far more complex.

Developmental psychologists tell us that value formation begins very early in life. Even before children are able to talk, they are able to sense neglect and indifference. They also learn how to manipulate parents and others into accommodating their every whim, if so allowed. It is just as important to teach small children the meaning of the word "no" as it is to shower them with love and compassion. Both love and limits are crucial ingredients for value formation.

The process of value formation continues as the years progress. Widely read Harvard child psychiatrist Robert Coles observes:

> Elementary school children need to learn how to get along with others, how to engage with them (in the tradition of the Golden Rule) as one would hope to be engaged by them; teenagers need to figure out how to regard their newly capable, yearning bodies and, too, the various interests and preferences and attitudes constantly being thrust upon them, by friends, by advertisements, by actors and actresses, announcers, singers and musicians, by sports heroes.[8]

If something of moral significance is to be posted on school bulletin boards, there is a strong case to be made for prominently displaying the Golden Rule, which admonishes us to "Do unto others as you would have others do unto you." But most important of all, if we are serious about promoting ethical values such as those expressed in the Golden

Rule, we must live in accordance with those values ourselves. That means treating others with respect and dignity rather than trashing them and their property. That means taking seriously what others have to say, just as we like to be taken seriously. That means including others in, just as we like to be included in. The best way to encourage children and adults alike to respect other people is to respect them. The best way to encourage children and adults to take others seriously is to take them seriously. The best way to teach others the importance of love and compassion is to treat them with love and compassion, even in situations when they aren't particularly lovable.

TOWARD A PUBLIC MORALITY

Any discussion of moral education in the classroom, particularly if it is a public school classroom, raises the question of what moral values should be taught. Similarly, any discussion of what moral standards should be written into law raises the question of what our public morality should be. Moral community and public morality are not quite the same thing, at least not as the terms are here being used. Moral community, as a continuing commitment to common values by two or more people, can exist in subgroups and subcultures. On the other hand, a *public morality*—here defined as common values that bind a society together—must enjoy a sufficient degree of consensus to provide useful reference points for public policy decisions such as the enactment of laws. Otherwise, the political process and legal system become nothing more than exercises in coercion, with those with the most clout carrying the day. All public moralities, it might be added, are moral communities. However, not all moral communities, some of which might involve only two or three people, are public moralities.

There are some matters—abortion, for example—about which we can do no more than agree to disagree. But if we look carefully beyond that which divides us, possibilities exist for identifying at least some values that at least some of us hold in common, values that we view as worthy of constituting a public morality. The very nature of ethical pluralism, of course, is such that we should not presume that these values are common to all of humankind, or, for that matter, even to all members of any particular society. That, however, should not preclude our looking for areas of agreement when such exist.

Three sets of values, each with deep roots in our political, religious, and other cultural traditions, merit careful consideration: (1) respect for persons, (2) integrity, and (3) compassion.

- *Respect for Persons.* Whether one looks at the Ten Commandments or more recent statements of rights such as our Declaration of Independence and our Bill of Rights, a persistent ethical theme in the cultural traditions that have been formative for this nation is the notion that we ought to respect other people. That means, among other things, respecting their physical integrity by refraining from doing things that injure them, respecting their property by refraining from destroying or taking what doesn't belong to us, and respecting their privacy by not snooping around where we have no business snooping around. When fully realized, respect for persons also involves acts of affirmation that transcend differences. This includes taking other people seriously and listening carefully to their views even when—some would say particularly when—they disagree with us. It means treating with dignity all persons, regardless of their national origins, racial or ethnic background, age, gender, sexual orientation, or anything else that is part of their identity as persons. Thus, respect for persons involves affirming diversity. In part, the answer to the question of how we can identify common values in a pluralistic society is that this can be accomplished to a significant degree by affirming and respecting diversity.[9]

- *Integrity.* While there are many differing views about which values should be taught in the classroom, I know no one who believes that cheating should be tolerated, let alone be respected. Even in a pluralistic society, there are some matters that ought to be beyond debate. Integrity is one of these matters. Being honest and keeping faith with other people—in business dealings, in marriage, and in many other contexts—are essential elements in any effectively functioning society. The heart and soul of integrity are captured in the phrase "being true"—being true to ourselves by acting in accordance with the ideals to which we are committed, and being true to others by maintaining fidelity in our relationships with them.[10]

- *Compassion.* It isn't enough just to respect people and be honest in our dealings with them. Compassion is also a necessary ingredient if the communities in which we live are to be anything more than collections of isolated individuals. Derived from the Latin words *com* (which means "together") and *pati* (which means "to suffer"), compassion involves, as the *Oxford English Dictionary* puts it, "fellow-feeling, sympathy."[11] In the sense that the term is here being used, compassion involves trying to get a sense of where others are coming from, trying to understand how it feels to be in their shoes. It involves recognizing their humanity and being responsive to their needs, while at the same time not precluding "tough love," which involves expecting that others behave in a responsible manner and not abuse charity. In a very basic sense, compassion is the delicate seasoning that brings warmth and understanding to community—indeed, the very ingredient that makes community possible.

There is room for debate about borderline situations with respect to each component of this trilogy of values—for example, the question of whether it is morally justifiable to steal food in order to feed one's starving family. In a society committed to human decency, however, the core values themselves ought to be beyond debate. If we can all agree that these core values are beyond debate, possibilities exist for identifying a public morality sufficiently inclusive to provide the moral fibers necessary to bind together a society such as ours. And under the umbrella of moral community provided by this public morality, it is both meaningful and appropriate to address questions of obligation pertaining both to ourselves and to our compatriots who join us in affirming the core values of this public morality.

THE ETHICS OF INTERVENTION

But what if the umbrella of moral community cannot be extended far enough to cover those contemplating acting in ways at odds with the values we affirm? What if a universally held public morality is not identifiable? In a pluralistic society, we must be prepared for this possibility—some would say this inevitability.

An ethical framework of humility does not automatically translate into a mandate for inactivity or for unlimited tolerance of anything and everything that anyone else might be inclined to do. For example, if we returned home one night to discover a burglar walking off with our CD player, it is unlikely that any of us would respond by saying to the burglar, "Quite obviously you and I have different values. But I respect where you are coming from." It is far more likely that we would call the police or otherwise try to prevent the burglar from stealing our property. The humility of faith, including a faith that demands of us love for our fellow human beings, does not preclude standing up for our own rights or protecting our own well-being.

Nor does the humility of faith preclude standing with others who are threatened and doing what we can to ensure their well-being. Indeed, a faith that affirms the dignity of all and that gives expression to justice and equality demands that we intervene in certain situations—and that we be willing to pay the price for intervention. Martin Luther King Jr. knew what it was to take a stand on principle and pay the cost for so doing. So also did Socrates, Dietrich Bonhoeffer, and many other heroic figures—some famous and justifiably so, others whose names never have appeared and never will appear in the annals of history.

There is in all this a very delicate balance to be maintained between taking action by standing with those who are threatened, on the one hand, and, on the other hand, succumbing to arrogance by attempting to impose our views on others. Sometimes it is very difficult to decide exactly where to draw the line of demarcation that distinguishes justifiable intervention from unwarranted intrusion. Physician-assisted suicide is a case in point. I personally have deep moral reservations about physician-assisted suicide. I believe that life is a gift from God that ought to be treasured and preserved. I also have considerable discomfort with the idea of physicians, who take an oath to preserve life, prescribing lethal drugs to be used to end life. Yet it is by no means apparent that those of us with moral reservations about physician-assisted suicide have any business using the legal machinery of government to prevent physicians from prescribing lethal drugs to be self-administered by terminally ill patients who wish to end their suffering by ending their lives. On the other hand, I have no reservations whatsoever about intervening to stop child abuse or about using the legal system to punish murderers and others who act in ways destructive of the well-being of our fellow human beings. And as already noted, I applaud the action taken by Martin Luther King Jr. and others who have taken a stand on principle to further the cause of justice.

More detailed discussion of the ethics of intervention must be reserved for other occasions. Suffice it to say here that the faith we affirm might well call upon us to stand with those who are threatened and to intervene in situations in which the well-being of others is at risk. This is true even in cases in which the umbrella of moral community does not extend far enough to cover the activity in question, the result being that in such situations we can act only on the basis of our individual affirmations of faith.

A CHALLENGE

By now, those who hoped to find a place on which to stand and move the whole world are probably very frustrated, while those who fancy that they have a God's-eye view of the truth are probably very unhappy with what has been said here. But sometimes what we want and what we can have are two very different things. Those who are dissatisfied with the arguments that have been presented here will undoubtedly characterize them as "incomplete" or "inadequate." That, however, would be to miss the point. The burden of proof is on those who believe that it is possible to go beyond mere belief and somehow prove or otherwise conclusively demonstrate that one set of values is indeed the correct set of values and that all conflicting sets are false or mistaken.

It is worth underscoring the fact that the arguments presented in this volume fully allow the possibility that there is an existing moral order in the universe. Indeed, I am among those who believe that such is the case. The underlying question, however, is whether there is any basis for making such a claim that goes beyond mere assertion of belief. In the course of the years, I have tried repeatedly to find such a basis only to be met with failure at every turn of the road on every path taken. It is incumbent on those who believe that there is a basis for claiming that there is an existing moral order in the universe that goes beyond mere assertion of belief to show how this can be done. I eagerly await their conclusions. In the meantime, I am content to approach value questions within the framework of an understanding of faith that acknowledges human finiteness, an understanding of faith leavened with a substantial measure of humility.

A VALLEY OF HOPE AND RENEWAL

The good news is that failure to find a place on which to stand and move the whole world does not doom us to meandering aimlessly in a valley of despair. Coming to grips with the limits of what we are able to do, however, does necessitate refocusing and redirecting our quest. Within the framework of the affirmations of faith that give form to our lives, we must wrestle as best we can with the question of what ought to count above all else, what ideals ought to inform our conduct, and what these affirmations bind us in conscience to do. And as we seek to identify public moralities capable of giving direction to the societies in which we live, we must reach out to others, seeking common ground in the valley in which we and those with whom we share earthly existence live. That's what ethics on the horizontal is all about. If we are willing to undertake this endeavor with openness, sensitivity, and understanding, we will discover that the valley in which we live is not a valley of despair but a valley of hope and renewal.

Ten Questions for Reflection and Discussion

1 Is a cohesive public morality possible in a pluralistic society?

2 What values do you believe ought to be part of a public morality?

3 How might we go about fostering these values?

4 What types of formative experiences ought we seek to provide for our children and others on whose lives we hope to have an impact?

5 What does respect for persons entail?

6 What does integrity involve? Is it possible to deceive other people while acting with integrity?

7 What does compassion involve? Why, if at all, should we be compassionate?

8 Why, if at all, should we tolerate the views of others?

9 What, if any, should be the limits of tolerance?

10 When, if at all, is intervention in the lives of others in order?

NOTES

1. Henry David Thoreau, "Civil Disobedience," in *Civil Disobedience: Theory and Practice,* ed. Hugo Adam Bedau (Indianapolis: Bobbs-Merrill, 1969), 28. Thoreau pays scant attention to the fact that along with the particular obligation to obey a law (if judged to be morally appropriate), it is also possible to talk about a general obligation to obey a law that stems from its being part of a legal system viewed as authoritative. Martin Luther King Jr., for example, deeply believed in the ideals given expression in our Constitution and legal system and believed that, generally speaking, one ought to comply with the law. However, he also believed that if a particular law was morally offensive, there was a diminished obligation to comply with it and even, as noted above in chapter 1, in some cases an obligation not to comply with it. When set against the backdrop of a general obligation to comply with the law stemming from a determination that the legal system of which it is a part possesses authority, determining that a particular law has appropriate moral content intensifies the obligation to comply with that law. *General obligation + particular obligation = even greater obligation.* On the other hand, if the moral judgments that one makes lead to the conclusion that there is no particular obligation to obey a particular law, the practical impact is to diminish or, if the law in question is highly offensive, override the general obligation to comply with the law. *General obligation - particular obligation = diminished obligation (or no obligation at all).* Even in a country run by a brutal dictator who rules in an arbitrary manner, there might still be an obligation to obey some laws. While there might be no general obligation to comply with the law in such a country, there still might be particular obligations to comply with particular laws—e.g., traffic laws that contribute to public safety.

2. *Oxford English Dictionary,* 2d ed., s.vv. "obligation," "ligament," "religion." Though many believe that *ligare* is the root of "religion," the etymology of religion is uncertain. Cicero believed that the Latin word for religion came from *relegere,* which means "to read again." Others have favored an etymology that connects the word religion with ligare, perhaps because they find appealing an interpretation of religion that carries with it the notion of being bound.

3. One of the more interesting—and difficult—rhetorical questions is the question of whether it is appropriate to appeal to values that one does not hold

when attempting to persuade others to do things that one thinks they ought to do. For example, suppose that someone who believes that we ought to give money to charity without expecting anything in return is involved in a fund drive for a social service organization that provides vital services for low-income families. Is it appropriate for the self-effacing fundraiser to appeal to the vanity of others by promising them that they will receive all sorts of public recognition for their good deeds? The answer to that question, of course, depends on the particular values that one affirms. My own view is that there is considerable loss of integrity if one appeals to values that one does not espouse to try to persuade others to do what one wants them to do, even if it is for a worthy cause.

4. Toulmin made this observation in a conversation with the author while in residence at the National Humanities Institute at the University of Chicago during the 1978–79 academic year.

5. Richard T. DeGeorge, *Business Ethics,* 4th ed. (Englewood Cliffs, N.J.: Prentice Hall, 1995), 48–59.

6. William Diehl, *Christianity and Real Life* (Philadelphia: Fortress Press, 1976), 55–56.

7. While many of us would readily agree that the Ten Commandments give expression to some very important ethical values that ought to be taken very seriously, we should not assume that the commandments provide a completely adequate definition of morality. As a matter of fact, some of the commandments have cultural overtones that are sharply at odds with values we hold dear today. Take, for example, the last of the commandments, which makes reference to slavery without in any way questioning it. Exod. 20.17 states, "You shall not covet your neighbor's house; you shall not covet your neighbor's wife, or male or female slave, or ox, or donkey, or anything that belongs to your neighbor." The following chapter lists rules specifying the way slaves should be treated. And have you noticed that the neighbor's wife is on the property list? Recall, for example, the story of how Jacob got married (Gen. 29.9–30). Rachel was to have been Jacob's wages for working seven years for her father, Laban. However, Laban, who had not taken a course in business ethics, gave Jacob Rachel's older sister Leah instead. Unfortunately for Jacob, the marriage had been consummated (the act of sexual intercourse finalized the transaction) before he discovered that he had been deceived. So he worked

for Laban for seven more years in order to get Rachel, which is how he ended up having two wives. Hardly a model for marriage (or business ethics) today!

8. Robert Coles, *The Moral Intelligence of Children* (New York: Random House, 1997), 169.

9. Affirming and respecting diversity, it should be emphasized, in no way implies abandoning one's own beliefs and perspectives. Indeed, if we were to abandon our own beliefs and perspectives when confronted with differing beliefs and were to accept the beliefs of others in an unreflective manner, it wouldn't make sense to talk about affirming and respecting diversity since diversity would no longer be present. Nor does respecting other people in any way commit us to respecting everything that they do. For example, an ethic of respect for persons in no way suggests that we ought to treat with respect the work of child pornographers or anything else detrimental to human well-being. The underlying point, however, is that even the child pornographer is a human being whom God has created, a person precious in God's eyes. While those of us committed to the notion of respect for all persons ought to despise the nefarious activities in which the child pornographer has engaged and support harsh punishment for such despicable behavior, that doesn't translate into despising the person who has done these terrible things. Difficult though it might be in the midst of our anger and anguish, it is still incumbent on us to respect the humanity of the child pornographer and refrain from engaging in abusive behavior directed toward that individual, even as we demand swift justice and appropriate punishment.

10. There is room for debate about the question of what keeping faith with other people means in certain situations. For example, suppose that a person with a terminal illness asks her doctor, "Am I going to be all right?" A friend who is an oncologist (and who is frequently asked this sort of question) states that if one is to keep faith with patients, it is important to try to understand what the patient is really asking and then respond to that question. Is it an inquiry about the brute facts of the illness? Or is it a request for comfort and assurance? My friend believes that it is often the latter and, when such appears to be the case, responds accordingly. In a book that was published several years ago, American theologian Paul Lehman recounts an occasion when he visited a friend who was terminally ill with cancer. He recalls that "when I saw her for the last time, as she lay upon her hospital bed, she said to me, 'What do the doctors say? Is there anything that can be done?'" Reflecting about this case,

Lehman observes, "The point at issue here is not the celebrated ethical question of the right of the patient to the truth. The point at issue is, granted that the patient has a right to the truth, what is the truth to which the patient has a right?" (Paul Lehman, *Ethics in a Christian Context* [New York: Harper & Row, 1963], 132–33).

11.   *Oxford English Dictionary,* 2d ed., s.v. "compassion."

INDEX

—

ABOUT THE AUTHOR

—

Daniel E. Lee teaches ethics at Augustana College, Rock Island, Illinois, where he has been a member of the faculty since 1974. Previous books include *Death and Dying: Ethical Choices in a Caring Community* (1983), *Hope Is Where We Least Expect to Find It* (1993), and *Generations and the Challenge of Justice* (1996). He writes a weekly column that appears in the op-ed sections of the *Rock Island Argus* and the *Moline* (Ill.) *Dispatch* as well as occasional pieces for other papers. Op-ed pieces he has written have appeared in *USA Today*, the *Chicago Tribune*, the *Chicago Sun-Times*, the *Journal of Commerce*, the *St. Louis Post-Dispatch*, the *Peoria Journal-Star*, and several other newspapers. In 1996 he joined the news team at WHBF-TV in Rock Island as political analyst. Social service activities include serving as adviser for the Augustana Habitat for Humanity campus affiliate and as member of the ethics committee for Alternatives for the Older Adult Inc.

Born in the mountains of Montana, he began his formal education in a two-room country school. A summa cum laude graduate of Concordia College, Moorhead, Minnesota, he received M.A., M.Phil., and Ph.D. degrees from Yale University. A U.S. Navy veteran, he served as a commissioned officer assigned to naval intelligence.